Brent Q. Hafen
Molly J. Brog

EMOTIONAL
SURVIVAL

A SPECTRUM BOOK

Prentice-Hall, Inc., Englewood Cliffs, N.J. 07632

Library of Congress Cataloging in Publication Data

Hafen, Brent Q.
    Emotional survival.

    "A Spectrum Book."
    Includes bibliographical references and index.
    1. Self-acceptance.   2. Self-respect.
3. Mental health.   4. Stress (Psychology).
5. Depression, Mental.   I. Brog, Molly J.
II. Title.
BF697.H323 1983   158'.1   82-18139
ISBN 0-13-274480-5
ISBN 0-13-274472-4 (pbk.)

This book is available at a special discount when ordered in bulk quantities.
Contact Prentice-Hall, Inc., General Publishing Division, Special Sales,
Englewood Cliffs, N.J. 07632.

10 9 8 7 6 5 4 3

ISBN 0-13-274480-5

ISBN 0-13-274472-4 {PBK.}

Editorial/production supervision by Maxine Bartow
Cover design © 1983 by Jeannette Jacobs
Manufacturing buyers: Cathie Lenard, Christine Johnston

Prentice-Hall International, Inc., *London*
Prentice-Hall of Australia Pty. Limited, *Sydney*
Prentice-Hall Canada Inc., *Toronto*
Prentice-Hall of India Private Limited, *New Delhi*
Prentice-Hall of Japan, Inc., *Tokyo*
Prentice-Hall of Southeast Asia Pte. Ltd., *Singapore*
Whitehall Books Limited, *Wellington, New Zealand*
Editora Prentice-Hall do Brasil Ltda., *Rio de Janeiro*

CONTENTS

ACKNOWLEDGMENTS

Grateful acknowledgment is extended for permission to use the following material:

Excerpts from *Essays on Self-Esteem* and *Building Self-Esteem*, both by L. S. Barksdale, are quoted with permission of copyright holder, L. S. Barksdale, Founder-President, The Barksdale Foundation for Furtherance of Human Understanding, Idyllwild, California.

Quotations from D. S. Viscott, *How to Make Winning Your Life Style*, quoted with permission of the author.

Charts and excerpts reprinted from *Executive Health* © 1978, by McGraw-Hill, Inc., New York, N.Y. 10020. All rights reserved.

The quote on page 110 is from "Psychological Mayhem," *Today's Health*, February 1974. Reprinted by permission of the publisher.

INTRODUCTION

Emotional survival.

Oh, it conjures up all kinds of visions! We think about mental health—we worry about "normalcy," wonder to ourselves whether we really fit into those neat little slots designed for the "stable."

We think, too, about the absence of mental health—the high-walled mental institutions, bars jutting across the windows, white-garbed technicians standing guard, the defeated shuffling across the sterile tile floor. We fear that someday we, too, may end up there.

Let's get a few things straight, right from the top.

There is no such thing as "normal," no one set of behaviors that sets us apart, no set of expectations that demands a conforming set of minds. Each of us is different; each of us reacts differently to the situation that faces us every morning as we rise from our beds.

If this is true, then how do we gauge emotional survival?

The answer is simple, yet complex.

It begins with our ability to love ourselves—our ability to respect ourselves, admire ourselves, forget our past mistakes, and look forward to the adventure of tomorrow. Emotional survival hinges on that perhaps more than on anything else.

The pages that follow will help you learn the skill of emotional survival. You'll learn what it means to love yourself. You'll realize, maybe for the first time, that it is *your* opinion that counts—not your mother's, not your husband's, not that of the family next door.

You'll find that self-esteem can be easily corroded, and you'll learn how to combat two of the biggest enemies: stress and depression. You'll learn how to help other people. And, most important, you'll learn how to reach out to yourself—how to recognize when you need help, and how to find it. You'll learn, finally, how to use support systems in your fight for emotional survival.

That survival, that essence of life, is within the reach of all of us. Begin now by taking the steps that will lead you there; the outline of those steps is here, free for the taking.

Express the greatest love for yourself, the best of emotional survival, by turning the page and beginning to read.

chapter one
HOW DO I LOVE ME?

How do I love me?

Not an easy question to answer for some; for others, an integral part of life. Your ability to love yourself—your measure of self-esteem—is your greatest tool for emotional survival.

Self-esteem is a result of those potentials (what you are) as well as those behaviors (what you can do) that are expressly appreciated by others—first parents, then peers. What happens when you realize the glaring discrepancy between your perception of yourself and the way you think you ought to be? Everyone has felt this discrepancy, and what happens to you at that moment depends a great deal on your basic sense of self-worth. If your sense of self-worth is usually high, you'll probably retain faith in yourself and bridge—or appreciably narrow—the gap. On the other hand, if your sense of self-worth is low, you'll probably become a victim of a self-fulfilling prophecy: You believe the negative inferences that others have made about you, and you eventually may make them come true.

Before you start reading this book, get a good idea of where you stand. Take the self-evaluation test that follows. You'll get a good idea of how much you love yourself. The results will guide you through the rest of this book and will make the journey much more meaningful.

SELF-ESTEEM EVALUATION*

Score as follows: 0 if not true; 1 if somewhat true; 2 if largely true; 3 if true.

1. I usually feel inferior to others.
2. I normally feel warm and happy toward myself.
3. I often feel inadequate to handle new situations.
4. I usually feel warm and friendly toward all I contact.
5. I habitually condemn myself for my mistakes and shortcomings.
6. I am free of shame, blame, guilt and remorse.
7. I have a driving need to prove my worth and excellence.
8. I have great enjoyment and zest for living.
9. I am much concerned about what others think and say of me.
10. I can let others be "wrong" without attempting to correct them.
11. I have a strong need for recognition and approval.
12. I am usually free of emotional turmoil, conflict and frustration.
13. Losing normally causes me to feel resentful and "less than."
14. I usually anticipate new endeavors with quiet confidence.
15. I am prone to condemn others and often wish them punished.
16. I normally do my own thinking and make my own decisions.
17. I often defer to others on account of their wealth or prestige.
18. I willingly take responsibility for the consequences of my actions.
19. I am inclined to exaggerate and lie to maintain a self-image.
20. I am free to give precedence to my own needs and desires.
21. I tend to belittle my own talents, possessions and achievements.
22. I am free to speak up for my own opinions and convictions.
23. I habitually deny, alibi, justify or rationalize my mistakes and defeats.
24. I am usually poised and comfortable among strangers.
25. I am very often critical and belittling of others.
26. I am free to express love, anger, hostility, resentment, joy, etc.
27. I feel very vulnerable to others' opinions, comments and attitudes.
28. I rarely experience jealousy, envy or suspicion.
29. I am a "professional people pleaser."
30. I am not prejudiced toward racial, ethnic or religious groups.
31. I am fearful of exposing my "real self."
32. I am normally friendly, considerate and generous with others.
33. I often blame others for my handicaps, problems and mistakes.

34. I rarely feel uncomfortable, lonely and isolated when alone.
35. I am a compulsive "perfectionist."
36. I accept compliments and gifts without embarrassment or obligation.
37. I am often compulsive about eating, smoking, talking or drinking.
38. I am appreciative of others' achievements and ideas.
39. I often shun new endeavors because of fear of mistakes or failure.
40. I make and keep friends without trying.
41. I am often embarrassed by the actions of my family or friends.
42. I readily admit my mistakes, shortcomings and defeats.
43. I experience a strong need to defend my acts, opinions and beliefs.
44. I take disagreement and refusal without feeling "put down", or rejected.
45. I have an intense need for confirmation and agreement.
46. I am eagerly open to new ideas and proposals.
47. I customarily judge my self-worth by comparison with others.
48. I am free to think any thoughts that come into my mind.
49. I frequently boast about myself, my possessions and achievements.
50. I accept my own authority and do as I, myself, see fit.

Scoring: To obtain your Self-Esteem Index, add the individual scores of all *even*-numbered statements (i.e., nos. 2, 4, 6, 8, etc.). From this total subtract the sum of the individual scores of all *odd*-numbered statements (i.e., nos. 1, 3, 5, 7, etc.). This *net score* is your *current* Self-Esteem Index, or SEI. For example: If the sum of all the individual scores of the even-numbered statements is 37 and the sum of all the individual scores of the odd-numbered statements is 62, your SEI is 37 – 62 or a *minus* 25. The possible range of one's Self-Esteem Index is from –75 to +75. Yours will fall somewhere in between. Do not be concerned about your SEI, no matter how low, or even *negative*. Remember, your self-esteem simply is what it *is*, the *automatic* product of your heritage and total life experience; and thus nothing to be ashamed or embarrassed about. It is important, however, that you be honest with yourself in order to obtain as valid a score as possible. For this score is a beginning reference point in gauging your progress in building self-esteem. Also remember that no matter how low your present SEI may be, you can bring it up to any desired value by conscientious effort.

   You may find comfort in the fact that lack of sound self-esteem is practically a universal problem that varies only in degree. It is, however, often so well camouflaged by false fronts and other protective devices that only a trained observer can detect it.

---

*L. S. Barksdale, *Building Self-Esteem* (Idyllwild, Calif.: The Barksdale Foundation, 1972), pp. 6–8.

Where do you go from here?

Start to make changes. They are important: The most critical aspect of good mental and emotional health is your ability to like and respect yourself. No value judgment is more important to you than the one you pass on yourself—not a conscious, verbalized judgment, but a feeling that can be difficult to isolate and identify because you experience it constantly.

"Our Self-Esteem is an emotion—not an intellectual inventory of our favorable characteristics, but how warm, friendly and appreciative we actually feel toward ourselves. It is the degree that we consciously or non-consciously accept and like ourselves, despite our mistakes and human frailties. It is not egotism!"[1] It is the individual's feeling about himself or herself as a person, a feeling that has profound effects on his or her emotions, desires, values, and goals.[2] "Our basic need and urge is to 'feel good' about ourselves, mentally, physically, and emotionally."[3]

> If I am not for myself, who will be?
>
> Ethic of the Fathers, *Talmud*

Self-concept, which is a big part of self-esteem, is not one entity. It is the "sum total of the view which an individual has of himself."[4] Everyone has feelings about himself or herself in the physical, intellectual, social, and emotional realms. In addition, the self-concept is made up of perceptions, attitudes, and ideas. Perceptions are sensory data about the self, whereas attitudes are emotionally toned ideas that are directed toward or against something. People direct attitudes toward others and in turn perceive others' attitudes toward them; this enters into their self-concept.

Experience and outside influences help forge the self-concept, and the self-concept helps determine the outcomes of various situations. Thus, every experience is given meaning by an individual's self-concept. "The self-concept is like an inner filter—every perception that enters the individual must go through the filter. As each perception passes through the filter, it is given meaning, and the meaning given is determined largely by the view the individual has of himself."[5]

Self-concept is formulated early in life. Parents have a large part in the developing self-concept of the child because they are the primary models with whom the child initially associates; parents are the primary feedback agents for the child's behavior and attitudes and the primary evaluators of the child's behavior. Even though self-concept can change throughout life, it is originally shaped and developed by the relationship between parent and child.

> The child is the crucible in which the concept of self-esteem is forged. And true self-esteem is . . . a confidence in one's own worth. A child's self-esteem develops out of contacts with significant others who communicate his worth to him in many ways. But a lack of this feeling can easily be engendered in a child by parents or others who continually make derisive remarks about him.
>
> Imagine, on the one hand, a child who is continually praised and encouraged by his parents for his many and varied efforts; and on the other hand, a child who is always berated, made fun of, and told of his stupidity. The former is likely to develop a feeling of confidence in his own capacities, while the latter may come to perceive himself as incompetent, inept, and worthless.
>
> Lou Benson

Just as self-concept is a vital part of self-esteem, so are self-confidence and self-respect. Self-confidence means that a person knows that he or she is competent to think, judge, and know; it doesn't permit that person to think that he or she is infallible. Self-respect indicates that a person feels a sense of self-worth. We all judge ourselves according to some standard, and whether or not we measure up to that standard determines our feelings of self-worth. It has been said that a "man makes himself worthy of living by making himself confident to live."[6]

No one should feel the need to prove his or her worth. Everyone has an innate worth, and "no one is one iota more or less worthy, more or less important than another" person.[7] Maxwell Maltz asserts that it is everyone's fundamental right to feel "as good as another [person] and that we are all children of God, born with rights to happiness and to the feeling that we are human beings of dignity. . . . Your greatness comes from your recognition of the best in yourself, from the human dignity that you give yourself, from the sense of self-respect that is your present to yourself from yourself every day of the year—not just on Christmas."[8]

> Before, I thought I was actually fighting for my own self-worth; that is why I so desperately wanted people to like me. I thought

their liking me was a comment on me, but it was a comment on them.[9]

Hugh Prather

Self-acceptance means liking the total you. In other words, you are worth as much as you think you are. Self-acceptance means the absence of complaint about yourself. "Complaining about yourself is a useless activity, and one which keeps you from effectively living your life."[10] Even though you should foster feelings of self-respect and self-acceptance, it is often easier and less risky to put yourself down than to build yourself up.

> A person who doubts himself is like a man who would enlist in the ranks of his enemies and bear arms against himself. He makes his failure certain by himself being the first person to be convinced of it.
>
> Alexandre Dumas

A self-accepting person has the following characteristics:[11]

- Actively participates in life
- Is objective and spontaneous
- Is emotionally and intellectually honest
- Understands problems that arise in life, and accepts his or her limitations in solving them
- Accepts the pleasure and discomforts that come with self-revelation
- Takes a reasonable view of life
- Is able to accept the limits of his or her talents and abilities, and to share in others' talents
- Doesn't brood about missed opportunities, lost causes, errors, and failures, but looks instead for the knowledge and experience they contribute to life
- Does not have irrational emotions
- Is able to endure solitude on a limited basis
- Can handle unconventionality at times, but not simply for the sake of rebellion
- Is not rigid with respect to rules
- Grants others their right to opinions and values
- Accepts, nourishes, trusts, respects, and loves self
- Has a genuine interest, caring, concern, and respect for self

To thine own self be true.
And it must follow as the night the day, thou canst not be false to
any man.

William Shakespeare

It's a pretty big order: Self-esteem encompasses accepting yourself,
nourishing yourself, trusting yourself, respecting yourself, and loving
yourself—that is, having a genuine interest, caring, concern, and respect for yourself.

There is no greater responsibility in the world than being a
human being and loving yourself. "To love oneself is to struggle to
rediscover and maintain your uniqueness."[12] Self-love means that you
love yourself without demanding the love of others; giving love to
others is directly related to how much you love yourself. Remember:
You cannot give that which you don't possess yourself.

So much is a man worth as he esteems himself.

François Rabelais

Inadequate self-esteem comes from an inappropriate awareness. Unfortunately, people become programmed by false and distorted concepts that cause them to feel inadequate. Typical sources of low self-
esteem include the following:

- Low parental esteem
- Belittling by parents, teachers, and peers
- Lack of appreciation expressed by parents, teachers, and peers
- Comparisons of children and their characteristics and talents by parents
- Lack of motivation to be independent
- False concepts given the individual by parents, teachers, and peers
- Demanding parents
- Parents that push children to fill needs that the parents never achieved
- Rivalry with an exceptionally talented brother or sister
- An unflattering physical appearance
- Adverse family, economic, social, cultural, and ethnic conditions
- Raising children on the basis of reward and punishment
- Overpossessiveness, overpermissiveness, and overcontrol
- A sense of guilt over affluence

- A high value being placed on material possessions
- Repeated defeats and failures
- Procrastination
- Lack of purpose in life
- Depending on others for a sense of worth
- Doing what comes easiest and never accepting challenges[13]

When people feel inadequate, they manifest symptoms of low self-esteem. A person with low self-esteem may have weight problems, a limp handshake, a weak voice, an unkempt appearance, postural problems, a frown, a lackluster appearance of the eyes, or a lack of eye contact when speaking to or interacting with others.

In terms of personality, a person with low self-esteem may suffer timidity, withdrawal or arrogance, a domineering attitude, or aggression; may display behavior that "masks" the real self with unnatural personality traits; may dominate conversation in social groups; may be demanding, critical, or rebellious; may be unable to admit mistakes or insecure; may compulsively smoke, drink, and talk; or may procrastinate.

Psychologically, someone with low self-esteem may be anxious, vacillating, unsure, absorbed with his or her problems, jealous, envious, suspicious, and self-hating, with a desire to be liked by everyone, to always be right, and to be recognized for his or her achievements.[14]

> Man's greatest fear is not of dying, but of feeling unfit to live.
>
> Nathaniel Branden

It's sometimes hard, amid constant challenges, to maintain a healthy respect and love for yourself, but some simple tactics can help.[15]

Learn the truth about yourself—but don't be brutal. You can build your self-esteem by increasing your awareness of your heritage and all of your life experiences. Take a little time for self-exploration by examining your thoughts, speech, desires, actions, needs, inner urges, compulsive drives, emotional reactions, moods, attitudes, values, concepts, assumptions, mistakes, defeats, and problems. Too many people overlook their successes and their attributes, concentrating instead on failures and weaknesses.

As you observe everything about yourself, don't condemn. Make sure that your truth about yourself is real, and that you acknowledge all of your good and positive qualities. If you find that you are always finding fault with yourself, your awareness may need to be reprogrammed. You need to "consciously generate positive feelings of self-esteem that will replace or cancel out old feelings of inferiority and inadequacy that have been accumulating at a non-conscious level since your earliest childhood."[16]

> A man's interest in the world is only the overflow of his interest in himself.
>
> George Bernard Shaw

Realize that there are three keys to self-esteem: You need to seek to identify your needs and strive to realize them; you need to try to find out who you are in relation to others; and you need to understand that there is a greatness in all people (both in yourself and in others).[17]

You should ask yourself, "Who am I really? How can I get in touch with my real self? How can I become myself?" Too often, we find ourselves living, thinking, feeling, and behaving as we assume others think we should rather than as *we* think we should. By doing this, we deny our real selves. Self-understanding has to start with you: You have to understand how to endow your own life with meaning. You must realize that you are as good as the next person, and that your needs are individual.

Keep your eyes on your goals despite discouragement, and project yourself into reality. Lose your fear of uncertainty and live with the fact that uncertainty will always exist. A person with self-esteem wrestles with uncertainties rather than denying them.

> Self-trust is the first secret of success.
>
> Ralph Waldo Emerson

Use your imagination and your ability to create mental pictures to plot out your future and to relive the situations where you were triumphant. Don't use your imagination to dwell on failures; relive successful situations until they blot out unsuccessful ones. Banish self-pity. Instead of storing fears and anxieties in your imagination, store moments of progress and courage.

Learn to relax. No one can keep up a constant, driving pace without becoming worn out and depressed. Take time out from your busy schedule to enjoy yourself and to ease stress and tension.

No one is perfect—and that includes you. Don't be chained to the past. Don't continue being the way you've always been just because you think you can't change. Forgive yourself for your past mistakes. Move forward now, and try harder, but don't let your past imperfections hold you back. "However you are, it's alright to be that way."[18] Understand that what a person really *is* is distinct from what he or she *does*; after all, "failure is simply someone else's opinion of how a certain act should have been completed."[19] If you wait to achieve perfection, you will find that you will not try anything that may result in failure. Doing is more important than succeeding; try something unconventional to add spice and an element of self-confidence to your life.

> If you ever doubt that perseverance can overcome obstacles, or that greatness is often preceded by adversity, consider this biographical sketch of a politician:
>
> > 1832: Lost job
> > 1832: Defeated for legislature
> > 1833: Failed in private business
> > 1834: Elected to legislature
> > 1835: Sweetheart dies
> > 1836: Nervous breakdown
> > 1836: Defeated for house speaker
> > 1843: Defeated for nomination to Congress
> > 1846: Elected to Congress
> > 1848: Lost renomination
> > 1849: Ran for land officer and lost
> > 1854: Defeated for Senate
> > 1856: Defeated for nomination for Vice-President
> > 1858: Defeated for Senate again
> > 1860: Elected President of the United States
>
> The politician was, of course, Abraham Lincoln.[20]
>
> Philip Goldberg

Discover the present you and all your possibilities. Don't engage in futile emotions such as guilt about what has been done or worry about what might be done.

Accept everything about yourself—I mean everything—not some things—everything. Every feeling, idea, hope, fear, smell, appearance—it is you and it is good. . . . You can do anything you choose to do; you can enjoy anything you choose to take part in, to be aware of. You are you and that is the beginning and the end—no apologies, no regrets—you are what you want—because you are you—and who can doubt that—who could want more— you have everything there possibly is—there is no more—you are everything—and you are so large and immense that you could never find the top or bottom—you will spend a lifetime enjoying the search—you will enjoy every minute—there is so much to know and experience within yourself.[21]

James A. Gold

Avoid labeling yourself. People often wrongly label themselves negatively, and they are sometimes wrongly labeled negatively by others. Labels can be leftovers from former days, times, and situations; they can program you for failure and keep you from a good deal of growth and pleasure. They can create a self-defeating pattern. Avoid using expressions that begin with "I'm _____ ," especially if they're negative.

The greatest evil that can befall man is that he should come to think ill of himself.

Goethe

Cultivate that winning feeling—the feeling and spirit that enable you to conquer hardships and move mountains. If you are able to cultivate such a feeling, it will pull you through crises when your equilibrium may be momentarily shaken.

Examine your habits. If you have bad ones, work on changing them. If you have good ones, continue them. Habits that harm you and that cause you to lose self-respect can seriously cripple your self-esteem and will continue to do so until they are changed.

If you alter your thoughts, your actions will change rapidly because your thoughts dictate your circumstances. Actively direct and control your thoughts; don't just passively avoid unpleasant thoughts.

Unmask your true feelings; learn to accept how you feel and to confront your emotions. You would never drive on a freeway at fifty-five miles an hour with a blindfold covering your eyes—nor should you speed through life with emotional blinders that may head

Bill of Rights for Winners

1. You have the right to be you—the way you are, the way you want to be.

2. You have the right to grow, to change, to become, to strive, to reach for any goal, to be limited only by your degree of talent and amount of effort.

3. You have the right to privacy—in marriage, family, or any relationship or group—the right to keep a part of your life secret, no matter how trivial or important, merely because you want it to be that way. You have the right to be alone part of each day, each week, and each year to spend time with and on yourself.

4. You have the right to be loved and to love, to be accepted, cared for, and adored, and you have the right to fulfill that right.

5. You have the right to ask questions of anyone at any time in any matter that affects your life, so long as it is your business to do so; and to be listened to and taken seriously.

6. You have the right to self-respect and to do everything you need to do to increase your self-esteem, so long as you hurt no one in doing so.

7. You have the right to be happy, to find something in the world that is meaningful and rewarding to you and that gives you a sense of completeness.

8. You have the right to be trusted and to trust and to be taken at your word. If you are wrong, you have the right to be given a chance to make good, if possible.

9. You have the right to be free as long as you act responsibly and are mindful of rights of others and of those obligations that you entered into freely.

10. You have the right to win, to succeed, to make plans, to see those plans fulfilled, to become the best you that you can possibly become.[22]

D. S. Viscott

you on a collision course. It's critical that you confront your feelings toward others so that you can honestly evaluate your feelings about yourself.

Learn to accept your weaknesses. You've probably isolated a few that have bothered you for years, but just because you are no good at math does not mean that you are not a good person, worthy of your respect and admiration. When temporary difficulties arise, do you blame yourself for your weaknesses and faults, deciding that you are a total failure? Change, and emphasize your positive characteristics instead.

Learn to accept yourself. Most people are never able to totally accept themselves—there are always new facets of the self that come with growth and that need acceptance. The great artist and sculptor Michelangelo created his statue *David* by chipping away everything that wasn't David. And that's what we must do—chip away and drop everything that isn't us. When we accept ourselves, we present our good side to others, and we have better feelings and acceptance toward others. This enables us to accept other people without fear of hurting ourselves.

> No one can make you feel inferior without your consent.
>
> Eleanor Roosevelt

Learn to maintain your worthy and happy self regardless of whether you solve life's problems. Sometimes you must merely learn to deal with your problems rather than solving them; recognize that problems are a part of the human condition, and don't measure your happiness by how few problems you have. You must realize that you have to deal with the world the way it is and the way you are.

> I am *somebody*! I may be poor—but I am *somebody*! I may be in prison—but I am *somebody*! I may be uneducated—but I am *somebody*!
>
> Reverend Jesse Jackson

Learn to laugh at yourself. Everybody makes mistakes, and you will, too, but you can't let them destroy your ability to move on and to achieve. Babe Ruth was one of the greatest baseball players who ever lived, yet if he had condemned himself every time he struck out, he would have destroyed his own confidence in his ability to play baseball at all.

Take five minutes each day to brag about yourself. Mention all your good qualities. Be specific. The Indian sage Meher Baba describes two kinds of perfection: a gradual change from the imperfect to the perfect, and the perfectness that exists now. With respect to the second

type of perfection, Baba states that no one in the world can be as perfect
a you as you are right now.[23]

> Every man has the right to feel that "because of me was the world
> created."
>
> *Talmud*

As well as verbalizing your positive attributes, you need to accept
compliments that others pay. Be assertive! Assertiveness increases
self-esteem: Do such things as greeting others, giving them compliments, using "I" statements, asking others for explanations of their
beliefs, expressing your own feelings spontaneously, expressing disagreement (in good taste when you don't agree with the views of
others), and holding eye contact.[24]

Follow your own instincts and desires. If you've always loved
animals and have wanted to be a veterinarian, don't go into accounting
just because criticism from friends and parents has driven you away
from veterinary science. If you're a man who's always wanted to be a
nurse, don't shy away from the profession just because everyone tells
you that only women should be nurses. Be yourself. Follow your
dream. You'll find that you will like yourself more and will have more
self-respect if you are true to yourself.

Set goals that will lead to a betterment of your self-esteem.
Examine your life and find out what's right about it; design goals that
will emphasize the positive aspects of your life. Determine the direction
that your life will take. You need to take the responsibility for your own
growth process, to imagine yourself being the actor instead of the one
acted upon. Remember: Don't say "I can't" when the truth is "I won't."

Determine what's missing from your life. What's keeping you
from having a really good feeling about yourself? Do you chronically
procrastinate? Are those extra few pounds that are hugging your hips
keeping you from meeting new people and trying new things? Set goals
that will help you change your shortcomings.

Start by making a list of the goals you have set. Keep the list
where you can see it every day (inside the cover of your chemistry
textbook, taped to the bathroom mirror, or next to the telephone in the
kitchen). You'll be able to assess the list each day and determine what

you've done toward meeting your goals; it will give you a sense of satisfaction and accomplishment. You'll start to like yourself better.

Be careful with goal setting: Done improperly, it can lead to frustration, despair, and disappointment instead of a sense of purpose and accomplishment. Stick to only a few goals at a time—no more than five. Perhaps you've got twenty-three goals you need to achieve; determine which two or three are most important to you right now, and go to work on those. Save the rest for later.

Be realistic in setting your goals. If you are thirty-four pounds overweight, don't expect to be at your ideal weight by Thanksgiving if fall is already nipping the air. If you and your sister have been fighting all your lives, don't expect to achieve a permanent peace; work, instead, on getting along just while you are home for spring break (when fighting and bickering upset your entire family).

Be specific. Don't jot down that you want to "lose weight"; instead, commit yourself, on paper, to "lose ten pounds by March 1." "Study calculus" won't bring as sure results as will "study calculus for fifteen minutes before calculus class." Write things down, and stick to your commitments.

Your self-esteem will improve greatly if you start doing nice things for yourself. Take time out from your classes, your part-time job, your volunteer work at the children's center, to do something you really like to do—play a game of tennis, read an interesting novel, take a nap. You do nice things for others you like, don't you?

> Be grateful for yourself. Yes, for yourself. Be thankful. Understand that what a man is is something he can be grateful for, and ought to be grateful for.[25]
>
> William Saroyan

Thinking of others and striving to meet their needs can help you escape preoccupations with your own shortcomings and failures. Try joining a service group, or make a goal of doing something nice for someone else each week—drive a handicapped classmate to campus, visit a mononucleosis victim at the student health center, write a letter to your parents expressing your appreciation, visit a nursing home, bake some cookies to take to your neighbor.

Nothing is a greater impediment to being on good terms with others than being ill at ease with yourself

Honoré de Balzac

Everyone needs to be cared for and understood; you can start by caring for and understanding yourself.

Sound easy?

Perhaps. But there are constant forces chipping away at the emotional base established by self-esteem—constant forces that cause us to look back, to glance over our shoulders.

Without these forces, life would be dull; we wouldn't exist, in fact. With these forces, life becomes a continual contest.

The forces? Stress and depression.

They claim thousands of victims each year; they destroy self-esteem in all its fragile stages. But you don't have to fall prey. Find out how by turning to the next chapter.

Notes

[1]L. S. Barksdale. *Essays on Self-Esteem*. Idyllwild, Calif.: The Barksdale Foundation, 1977, p. 41.

[2]Maxwell Maltz. *The Magic Power of Self-Image Psychology* © 1964 by Dr. Maxwell Maltz. Englewood Cliffs, N.J. 07632: Prentice-Hall, 1964, pp. 199–204.

[3]L. S. Barksdale. *Building Self-Esteem*. Idyllwild, Calif.: The Barksdale Foundation, 1972, p. 15.

[4]Donald W. Felker. *Helping Children to Like Themselves*. Minneapolis, Minn.: Burgess, 1974, p. 2. Reprinted by permission of the publisher.

[5]Felker, p. 9.

[6]Nathaniel Branden. *The Psychology of Self-Esteem*. New York: Bantam, 1970, p. 114.

[7]Barksdale, p. 94.

[8]Maltz, p. 16.

[9]Hugh Prather. *I Touch the Earth, the Earth Touches Me*. New York: Doubleday, 1972.

[10]Wayne W. Dyer. *Your Erroneous Zones*. New York: Avon Books, 1976, p. 51.

[11]Eugene C. McDonald, Bert Kruger Smith, and Robert L. Sutherland. *Self-Acceptance*. Austin, Tex.: University of Texas Printing Division, 1973, pp. 15–16.

[12]Leo Buscaglia. *Love*. New York: Fawcett Books Group—CBS Publications, 1972, p. 138.

[13]Barksdale, pp. 9–10.

[14]Barksdale, pp. 8–9.

[15]Maltz, pp. 199–204.

[16]Barksdale, p. 30.

[17]Maltz, p. 17.

[18]Victor Daniels and Laurence J. Horowitz. *Being and Caring*. Palo Alto, Calif.: Mayfield Publishing Company, 1976, p. 6.

[19]Dyer, p. 133.

[20]Philip Goldberg. *Executive Health*. New York: McGraw-Hill, 1978, p. 112.

[21]James A. Gold, in Clark E. Moustakas. *Finding Yourself, Finding Others*. Englewood Cliffs, N.J.: Prentice-Hall, 1974.

[22]D. S. Viscott. *How to Make Winning Your Life Style*.

[23]Daniels and Horowitz, p. 10.

[24]Daniel A. Girdano and George S. Everly, Jr. *Controlling Stress and Tension: A Holistic Approach*. Englewood Cliffs, N.J.: Prentice-Hall, 1979, p. 144.

[25]William Saroyan. *Human Comedy*. New York: Harcourt Brace Jovanovich, Inc., 1971.

chapter two
SURVIVING STRESS

"That scared the life right out of me!" "He makes me sick." "That accident took ten years off my life!" "She gives me a pain in the neck."

Meaningless sayings?

No.

A frightening experience, one that evokes severe enough emotions, *can* cause death. Facing a person who leads us to feel rejected or who causes us to feel uncomfortable *can* make us sick (most often causing respiratory problems or the common cold). The stress caused by an accident *can* age you. Dealing with an unpleasant person *can* cause neck pains.

Although good self-esteem is the solid base for emotional survival, two villains can chip away at its strength. One is depression. The other, more profound factor is stress—the way our bodies react to physical, chemical, or emotional changes.[1] Those changes—physical, emotional, or chemical—cause physical or emotional tension, otherwise known as *stress*.

Each of us is under stress all of the time. Some stress is relatively minor (Did I remember to put a nickel in the parking meter? Did I unplug the iron before I left the house?), while some stress is severe (Will I lose my job over that bad report? Is my wife going to die from complications of her surgery? Is my husband going to file for divorce?).

Stress can be either long-term or short-term. Every biological organism experiences short-term stress. In short-term stress, you experience a stressful situation, you learn to adapt to it, and your life returns to a normal or near normal condition. Most people can take short-term stress and still maintain equilibrium most of the time.

George Sheehan refers to long-term stress as "the full-court press of life."[2] In times of long-term stress, there is no clear resolution of the stress, and no real return to equilibrium. One stressful situation follows another with no return to a normal lifestyle between situations. Long-term stress cannot be tolerated, and it usually results in complete nervous exhaustion of some type such as a nervous breakdown or some type of mental illness.

> Stress is any action or situation that places heavy or conflicting demands upon you that upset your body's equilibrium or the normal flow of daily activities.[3]
>
> Rosalind Forbes

All stress—whether minor or severe—has an effect on your body. Stress is, literally, the response of the body to any demand that is made upon it.[4]

Once it's under stress, the body reacts—physiologically as well as emotionally—to try and normalize things again. The wear and tear of stress takes its toll: As many as 80 percent of all people who go to doctors do so because of stress-related illnesses.[5] In fact, some doctors think that *all* illnesses, at least in part, are caused by stress.

But none of us could survive in an environment totally free of stress, either. A group of athletes were forced to lie on their beds for two weeks; none could engage in any activity at all. Their internal organs and their circulatory systems began to suffer lower performance levels; at the end of the two weeks, their muscles had started to soften and their bones had started to deteriorate.[6]

Actually, then, stress is an integral part of our ability to exist, to function, to grow, and to progress; without stress, our environment contains no challenge and no opportunity for growth. Stress is necessary—but "stress becomes dangerous when it is unduly prolonged, comes too often, or concentrates on one particular organ of the body."[7] The key, then, rests in learning to cope effectively with stress and in taking measures to reduce stress when it becomes severe. "It's a matter of learning to manage *it* [stress], rather than letting it control *you*."[8]

> Stress is a part of life, a part of living. It energizes and motivates behavior. In fact, mild or moderate forms of stress are actually essential to life. Dr. [Hans] Selye cautions, "Don't try to avoid stress. It is the very salt and spice of life. But do learn to master and use it." Stress is neutral. It is our reaction to it which determines whether it can be beneficial or harmful.[9]
>
> Rosalind Forbes

WHAT CAUSES STRESS?

Each of us is an individual, and each of us reacts to different situations in a different way. Even with the greatest respect for those differences, though, there are certain situations in life that tend to bring on stress.

Stress can result from negative things, such as divorce, death, or illness, but it can also be the result of positive things, such as getting married, winning in an athletic contest, receiving a promotion at work, or being recognized for an outstanding achievement.

Negative stress (known as *distress*) results from an increase in stress and produces a decrease in health and performance. On the other hand, positive stress (often referred to as *eustress*, signifying success and euphoria) also results from an increase in stress, but it usually produces increased health and performance.[10]

Your mind can distinguish between positive (or "good") and negative (or "bad") situations and stresses, but your body can't: Your body reacts the same way to both types of stress.

> There is such a thing as pleasant stress, as in the case of the Olympic winner at the moment of glory, or a conductor as his orchestra performs particularly well. They are just radiating excitement, and they are secreting all the stress hormones exactly the same as if they were dejected or had just heard of a death in the family.
>
> Hans Selye

EVALUATION OF STRESSFUL EVENTS*

Read the following list; place a checkmark next to each event that has happened to you during the past twelve months and record the event value indicated. The total score at the end will give you a good idea of where you stand.

100 Death of spouse
 73 Divorce
 65 Marital separation
 63 Jail term
 63 Death of close family member
 53 Personal injury or illness
 50 Marriage
 47 Fired from job
 45 Marital reconciliation
 45 Retirement
 44 Change in health of family member
 40 Pregnancy
 39 Sexual difficulties
 39 Gain of new family member
 39 Business readjustment
 38 Change in financial state
 37 Death of a close friend
 36 Change to a different line of work
 35 Change in number of arguments with spouse
 31 Mortgage over $10,000
 30 Foreclosure of mortgage or loan
 29 Change in responsibilities at work
 29 Son or daughter leaving home
 29 Trouble with in-laws
 28 Outstanding personal achievement
 26 Wife begins or stops work
 26 Begin or end school
 25 Change in living conditions

24 Revision of personal habits
23 Trouble with boss
20 Change in work hours or conditions
20 Change in residence
20 Change in schools
19 Change in recreation
19 Change in church activities
18 Change in social activities
17 Mortgage or loan less than $10,000
16 Change in sleeping habits
15 Change in number of family get-togethers
15 Change in eating habits
13 Vacation
12 Christmas
11 Minor violations of the law

Scoring: If your score is 300 or more, you have an 80 percent chance of developing a serious stress-related illness within the next two years. Similar severe illnesses will be suffered by 53 percent of those whose scores were 250–300, and by 33 percent of those whose scores were 150–200. (*Stress-related illness* refers to any illness that can be affected by stress; such illnesses include asthma, cancer, and heart failure. It has been estimated that 80 percent of all those who see doctors do so because of stress-related illnesses; many doctors now believe that *all* illness is caused, at least in part, by stress.) There you have it—an accurate rundown of what, in the past year, may have contributed to your stress.

---

*Thomas H. Holmes and Minoru Masuda, "Psychosomatic Syndrome," *Psychology Today*, April 1972. Reprinted from *Psychology Today* Magazine, © 1972 Ziff-Davis Publishing Company.

Sometimes simply *anticipating* a stressful situation (like taking an exam or going to the dentist) can, in itself, produce tension. This kind of anticipation is what caused you to lie awake all night before you started your new job or before you competed in the golf tournament. Anticipatory stress can be worse than the actual stressful event.

> Taking it [a stressful situation] is not as bad as anticipating it; you don't have to worry while you are doing it.
>
>   Meyer Friedman and Ray Rosenman

Many causes of stress are unavoidable. You can't control your mother's death from leukemia, nor can you prevent an earthquake that destroys your small town and necessitates a move to a nearby city during reconstruction. Other causes of stress *are* avoidable, though: If you get nervous and upset in crowds, avoid them. Do your Christmas shopping early, and watch the football game on television instead of fighting the crowd at the stadium. If violent movies cause you a great deal of upset, don't go to them. Avoid stress where you can, and it will be easier for you to cope in those instances when you *can't* avoid stress.

Review the list of factors that are known to cause stress, as indicated in the Evaluation of Stressful Events. Think of ways you can reduce your own stress. For instance, if you recently got married and your wife is pregnant, you would probably be better off not buying a house right away—especially if buying the house would mean moving to a different town or assuming a large mortgage. If you were recently divorced, think twice before you change your job, move to a new community, go back to school, or enter a new relationship that might involve sexual intimacies—all situations that can add significantly to the stress of the divorce.

One final consideration is important: Your occupation can have a great deal to do with the amount of stress you suffer.[11] Jobs with exceptionally high levels of stress include laborer, secretary, inspector, clinical laboratory technician, office manager, foreman, manager or administrator, waitress or waiter, machine operator, farm owner, mine operative, painter (not artist), machinist, mechanic, structural metal worker, plumber, electrician, meat cutter, salesperson, public relations representative, police officer, firefighter, member of the clergy, social worker, therapist, nurse, nurse's aide, hospital orderly, health aide, dental assistant, and health technician.

People in some occupations suffer very few stress-related disorders; those occupations include sewer worker, examiner or checker, stock handler, artisan, maid, farm laborer, heavy equipment operator, freight handler, packer or wrapper, child care worker, college or university professor, labor relations representative, personnel administrator, and auctioneer or huckster.

You'll suffer the least amount of stress if you have the support of supervisors and colleagues, if your responsibilities are well suited to your skills, if you are being paid fairly for your work, and if you have authority consistent with the amount of responsibility you are given.

SIGNS OF STRESS

Various physical and mental signs can signal the onset of stress. To find out where you stand, take the Stress Evaluation Test on the next page.

What are other signs of stress?

Watch for increased cholesterol levels in your blood (determined by a laboratory test), excess weight for your height and age, a tendency to faint easily, a fear of sexual intercourse, fainting spells preceded by nausea, an inability to remain asleep throughout the night, muscle spasms, a feeling of fullness without eating, or a need to take aspirin or other medication daily.

Perhaps even more telling are the other mental and emotional symptoms of severe stress:

- Constant feeling of unease
- Inability to cry
- Tendency to burst into tears at slight or no provocation
- Feelings of self-destruction
- Impatience
- Tendency to be extremely critical of others
- Meticulousness about surroundings and possessions
- Tendency to be a perfectionist
- Tendency to lose temper

STRESS EVALUATION TEST

Place a checkmark next to any symptom or sign that you have had consistently during the past three months.

Loss of appetite
Overeating
"Butterflies" in the stomach
Fluttering of the eyes
Eyestrain
Tight neck muscles
Tight jaw muscles
Thrusting out of chin
Grinding of teeth
Sweating palms
Cold hands
Rapid pulse
Tightness of general body muscles resulting in jerky movement
Irregular breathing
Shallow breathing
Strained voice
Tight shoulder muscles, resulting in a hunching posture
Rigid spine
Tight forehead muscles
Tight muscles in fingers, resulting in tightly curled fingers
Headache
Nervousness
Body twitching
Trembling
Dryness of mouth
Tendency to be easily startled or frightened
Loss of sex drive
Impotence or loss of ability to respond sexually
Menstrual disorders or problems

Intestinal disturbances (including nausea, belching, diarrhea, constipation, or indigestion)
Increased use of alcohol, tobacco, or drugs
Weakness
Dizziness
Difficulty in sleeping or in falling asleep
Trouble sitting still
Trouble maintaining a physically relaxed position
Depression
Irritability
Tendency to tire easily
Sighing
Desire to hide
Strong urge to cry
Impulsive behavior incompatible with normal patterns of behavior
Vague feelings of anxiety
Difficulty in thinking clearly
Difficulty in making decisions
Difficulty in solving problems
Loss of the joy of living
Thoughts of killing yourself

Scoring: If you checked five or more of the signs and symptoms, you may be suffering from excess stress. No one will manifest *all* of these symptoms, nor are all the symptoms of extreme stress listed here. These are just the most common. Remember that we're talking about consistent symptoms—a gassy, upset stomach that bothers you night and day for months—not just an occasional spell of slight indigestion.

- A sense of suppressed anger
- Feelings of mild panic
- Frustration and concern over health
- Fear of death (your own and others')
- Fear of disease (especially cancer and heart disease)
- Fear of insanity or mental illness
- Fear of being alone
- Inability to cope with criticism
- Inability to get along with others
- Inability to concentrate for any length of time or to finish one job before another is started
- Feeling of separation or removal from people and things that once were important and vital
- A tendency to live mostly in the past
- Boredom
- Inability to freely express emotion, especially anger
- Feeling of rejection by family members
- Feeling of failure as a parent
- Inability to confide problems or concerns in another person
- Recurring feelings of not being able to cope with problems and frustrations
- Inability to have a really good laugh
- A feeling that you are being rejected by your family or that family members don't care about you
- A sense of despair about being an unsuccessful parent
- Dread as the weekend approaches
- Reluctance to take a vacation either alone or with your family
- A feeling that you cannot discuss problems with anyone
- Phobias (such as heights or enclosed spaces)

Four or more physical or mental health symptoms also qualify you for the high-risk category and may make it necessary to seek additional professional help.[12]

WHO IS MOST PRONE TO STRESS?

To find out whether your personality makes you prone to stress, take the following self-evaluation test.

PERSONALITY TRAIT SELF-EVALUATION TEST

Read over the list of personality traits, and place a check next to those traits that best describe you.

I get impatient when events move slowly.

I am generally not interested in what is going on around me.

I am eager to compete.

I can accomplish many different things at the same time.

I bring work home from my job.

I set deadlines and schedules.

I feel guilty if I relax and "do nothing."

I have a driving, forceful personality.

I speak and move at a quick pace.

I eat quickly.

I am achievement-oriented.

I am constantly striving for advancement in my career or for success in some hobby or sport.

I have a strong need for success.

I like to finish jobs quickly and move on to something else.

I am anxious while speaking, and don't finish my sentences.

I need to have public recognition.

I get angry easily.

I am number-oriented—I like to *count* my achievements and possessions.

I have aggressive or hostile feelings, especially toward people who are competitive.

I am not very observant.

I accomplish many things.

I am anxious about social advancement.

I try to do two or more things at once.

I am extremely time- and deadline-conscious; I become upset if things do not go on schedule.

Scoring: If you checked the majority of the traits, you are a Type A personality, and are much more apt to develop stress-related illnesses than if you checked fewer than half of the traits.

Type A personality.   You're simply more prone to stress if you are a Type A personality.

A Type A person is extremely competitive, is schedule- and time-oriented, and tries to stuff more work into less time. Extremely concerned with success and social acceptance, Type A personalities move and speak quickly, sometimes forgetting to finish the ends of sentences. They set several goals for themselves at once, and are rarely content with working on just one project at a time; strictly punctual, they are extremely concerned with coming out on top.

They are constantly in motion and appear outwardly confident and self-assured; inside, they are insecure. They feel guilty when relaxing because they fear slowing down. A Type A person not only lacks the ability to cope adequately with stress—the Type A person *creates* stress by the way that he or she lives and behaves.

Type B personality.   If you checked fewer than half of the responses in the Personality Trait Self-Evaluation Test, you're a typical Type B— easygoing, able to see things in a longer perspective, realistic about what you can achieve, relatively unworried about the future.

Type B personalities are less concerned with schedules; they are able to make decisions easily, are content with taking a longer time to achieve goals, and are seldom impatient. They fare much better healthwise than their uptight brothers and sisters!

Some factors in your personality are beyond your control; with help, you *can* learn to overcome and control others. Learn to reduce your overload of frustration and to lengthen your effective achieve-ment span if you're a Type A; most critical of all, eliminate what stress you can and strive to cope with the stress you can't get rid of.

HOW THE BODY REACTS TO STRESS

Whenever it is threatened in any way, the body prepares for the "fight." In a strict medical sense, stress is anything that triggers the body's adaptive mechanisms—anything that helps the body get ready to pro-tect itself by causing these reactions to occur. The reactions that enable us to cope with stress or to meet a stressful situation are the same ones that enable us to run from an approaching automobile that is about to run us over, to fight off an attacker, to chase a bus, to lift a fallen tree off the body of a young child.[13]

The physical reactions to stress that make the body speed up to confront or escape threatening situations include the following:

1. The cerebral cortex, located in the brain, sends impulses along a complicated network of nerves that interact to create a state of preparedness in the body.

2. The heart pumps faster and with stronger beats, circulating the blood more efficiently to provide additional fuel for the body.

3. Skeletal muscles, especially those required for quick motion or for lifting or pushing, contract and become filled with oxygenated blood, preparatory for motion. These muscles tense in readiness for confrontation of the stress.

4. With increased circulation, there is more blood and therefore more oxygen to the brain, which stimulates the thought processes.

5. Blood pools in the trunk and the head, which means that there is less blood in the extremities.

6. The spleen contracts, forcing increased blood circulation.

7. Eyesight is sharpened by impulses sent from the cerebral cortex along the optic nerve.

8. The sense of smell is sharpened by impulses sent from the cerebral cortex along the olfactory nerve.

9. The adrenal glands are stimulated, causing the secretion of large amounts of adrenalin.

10. Blood vessels in the skin are stimulated to contract, resulting in a reddening of the skin (especially in the facial area, causing a flushing of the face during extreme fear or anger).

11. Further stimulation of the adrenal glands, especially the adrenal medulla, causes a heightening of blood sugar, resulting in a quick burst of energy.

12. The airways leading to the lungs and the air passages in the lungs dilate, allowing for the deep breathing necessary in vigorous physical activity.

13. Red blood cells flood the bloodstream so that more oxygen is carried to the muscles in the limbs and to the brain.

14. The pupils dilate to improve vision.

15. The pituitary gland signals the endocrine system to speed up hormone production.

16. Chemicals released in the skeletal muscles act to reduce muscle fatigue and allow the muscles to sustain long-term rigorous activity without giving out.

17. Chemicals that enter the bloodstream accelerate the coagulating func-

tion of the blood (if the body is injured, the blood will clot much more rapidly).

18. Nerve impulses sent from the cerebral cortex along the pelvic nerve (sacral parasympathetic nerve) signal the bladder and bowels to evacuate—which is why some people lose control of their bladder and bowels during extreme fear.

The most telling indications that the fight-or-flight response is turned on *right now* are these:

Rapid pulse
Increased perspiration
Pounding heart
Tightened stomach
Tensing of muscles in arms and legs
Shortness of breath
Gritting of teeth
Clenching of the jaw
Inability to sit still
Racing thoughts
Excessively gripping emotions[14]

                                                            Philip Goldberg

These reactions on the part of the body enable us to lash out at an attacker—to see and smell more acutely, to keep punching or running for a longer period of time, to breathe more rapidly, to avoid bleeding severely from an injury. But the person who has just been told that he or she did not get an expected pay raise goes through much the same physical reaction, with no way to vent rage, no way to express the body's preparedness. Because there is no avenue of physical expression, the body undergoes tremendous wear and tear. It needs to be relieved of this fight-or-flight response or chronic stress results. Chronic stress may in turn cause the breakdown of the body.

STRESS AND DISEASE

In some instances, stress is short-lived; the stress-provoking situation is removed or is resolved, and you are able to move on without feeling many ill effects from your bout with it. In other instances, however, the stress is of extreme duration (sometimes for a lifetime, with a person who is born without arms or legs, or sometimes for many years, with a young woman who divorces early in her marriage and never remarries). In those situations, the ongoing stress literally *wears out* the body. One of the most significant ways in which it wears out the body, of course, is by causing disease.

Disease originally meant a lack of ease—not an illness.[15] Today, that concept still holds true: Those who are not at ease—who are suffering the effects of stress—are those who are likely to sicken.

Medical researchers who finally unraveled the puzzle of disease by discovering that germs cause illness failed to solve one final, critical riddle: What causes the onset of disease? Since then, we have discovered something that challenges all of our previous ideas about disease: Events of ordinary life, such as marriage, a vacation, a new job, or a personal achievement, can help trigger illness, because the effort that is required to cope with these life events weakens our resistance.[16]

> Virtually all illness has an emotional component.[17]
>
> Howard R. and Martha E. Lewis

Emotions can alter the body's hormone balance, change the blood supply and blood pressure, inhibit digestion, and change breathing patterns and skin temperature.

In other words, stress causes disease.

How? Disease development requires three conditions: (1) the presence of a bacteria, a virus, or some other disease-causing agent; (2) a host tissue in the body that can be affected by the disease-causing agent (the lung tissue, for example, can be affected by viral pneumonia); and (3) an external or internal factor that lowers the body's resistance to the disease-causing factor. In the presence of disease-causing agents, stress provides the third critical key: It lowers the body's ability to resist disease and infection.

You've already started to pinpoint your own risk of stress-related diseases. Do you want to find out even further where you stand? You can calculate your own risk by taking the following tests. Answer honestly, following all directions and keeping accurate score.

LIFESTYLE EVALUATION

Assess yourself in relation to each of the following statements. If the statement is true of your lifestyle, give yourself the score indicated for that statement. Total your score after you have assessed all statements listed.

+2 You felt good yesterday.

+1 You felt only so-so yesterday.

+0 You were ill yesterday.

+1 You did not take any medication yesterday—not even aspirin for a headache.

+1 You have not had any illnesses during the last month—not even a cold or the flu.

+1 You have not had any accidents during the last month—not even a minor scrape or scald.

+2 You were pleasantly tired last night when you went to bed.

+1 You were overtired last night when you went to bed.

+0 You were exhausted last night when you went to bed.

+1 You slept well last night.

+1 You did not spend more than one hour last night watching television, reading a book, or staring blankly into space.

+1 You practice yoga or some other form of meditation.

+1 You set some time aside every night for a hobby or for some other form of relaxation.

+2 You are less than thirteen pounds overweight.

+1 You are less than twenty-six pounds overweight.

+0 You are more than twenty-six pounds overweight.

+1 You take one spoonful or less of sugar in your coffee or tea.

+1 You eat less than eight ounces of butter each week.

+1 You average less than two large glasses of beer or a shot of liquor a day.

+2 You get more than an hour of vigorous exercise each week.

+1 You get half an hour to an hour of vigorous exercise each week.

+0 You get less than half an hour of vigorous exercise each week.

+1 You participate in sports.

+1 Your job is not at a desk.

+1 You spent quality time with someone you love last week.

+2 You do not smoke.

+1   You smoke less than ten cigarettes a week.
+0   You smoke more than ten cigarettes a week.
+1   You have not smoked for more than five years.
+1   You do not smoke a pipe.
+1   You do not smoke cigars.

Scoring: Add your score, and multiply the total by 4. If the result after multiplication is 0 to 25, your lifestyle is poor, and you are probably not healthy enough to cope with mild stress adequately. If your score is 25 to 50, you still need some improvement. A score of 50 to 75 indicates that your lifestyle is reasonably good, and you are probably healthy enough to withstand mild stress. If your score is 75 to 100, your lifestyle is excellent. You are probably healthy enough to cope adequately with brief periods of severe stress. The healthier you are, the more you improve your chances of being able to deal with stressful situations without sustaining residual harm.

PERSONALITY INDICATOR

Using 5 as an average on each of the following statements as they apply to you, score yourself from 0 to 10 on each statement. Total your score.

1. You are eager to compete.
2. You have a personality that is forceful and driving.
3. You strive for advancement on the job or for success in sports.
4. You like to get things done quickly.
5. You get impatient when you are delayed or held back.
6. You are time- and deadline-conscious.
7. You are anxious for social advancement.
8. You are anxious for public recognition.
9. You can accomplish many different activities.
10. You get easily angered over people or things.

Scoring: If your score is under 50, you are probably able to deal relatively well with stress. If it is over 50, you are probably not able to deal very well with stress; your risk of having a heart attack is three times higher than if you had scored under 50.

By now, you've got a pretty good indication of where you stand. And believe this: Stress *does* cause disease. The results of one fascinating study serve to bear out that hypothesis. A group of patients who reported to a doctor with symptoms of a cold or nasal infection were asked to return to the same doctor when their symptoms had disappeared. As each patient returned to the doctor, the doctor measured the patient's freedom of breathing, amount of swelling in the nasal passages, amount of secretion in the nose, and blood flow. Each was pronounced recovered. The doctor then started to talk to the patient about the event or events that occurred just prior to the onset of the illness—a man's acceptance of a new position with his company, the week-long visit of a woman's mother-in-law, or the death of a close friend, for example. Then the doctor repeated the same physiological tests.

Amazingly, the cold symptoms had returned. By simply *talking about* the stress-provoking situations, the doctor had caused a recurrence of a disease in a completely healthy person! Nasal tissue biopsies confirmed that actual tissue damage had occurred during the discussion of the stressful situation.[18]

The feelings of anxiety, hostility, and conflict that accompany stress bring about actual physical changes, as discussed earlier. Stress can alter body chemistry and organ function, but if we are in good health and living a well-balanced lifestyle, we have the capacity to restore ourselves to a state of equilibrium. In other words, if we're in good shape physically and emotionally, we can bounce back easily from periods of brief stress without feeling any ill effects.[19]

What happens when the stress is severe, prolonged, inescapable, or intensified? Or what happens if we are not in good health physically and emotionally? Just the opposite: The stress causes very real and severe physical and emotional harm. Our body's efforts to normalize itself are frustrated, and disease and illness result.

PAIN

Pain, a sensory signal indicating that the body's state of normality is being threatened or disrupted,[20] is perceived in much the same way as sights, sounds, smells, and tastes are perceived: It involves the stimulation of nerves, and it is accompanied by an emotional response of varying magnitudes.[21]

Stress affects not only the development of pain, but the perception of and sensitivity to pain. A person who is rigid, goal-oriented, and forceful in personality—a Type A person—will perceive pain as being more intense than will a more easygoing person (a Type B person). Pain that may practically turn a Type A person into a bed-bound invalid may be merely noticed and tolerated by a Type B person.

There are physiological changes as well. Under stress, the chemical responsible for lowering the pain threshold cannot be retained by normal blood platelets, and the victim perceives pain more intensely.[22] In addition, the chronic depression that is a result of severe stress has been shown to be the precursor to most chronic pain conditions.

STRESS AND SUDDEN DEATH

Overwhelming stress may be caused by deep personal loss (such as death of a spouse), situations involving personal danger, or situations involving intense relief; if it cannot be ignored, evokes intense emotions, and is beyond an individual's control, it can and sometimes does cause sudden death.[23]

Several factors are responsible for the phenomenon of sudden death due to stress:

Hopelessness. In an experiment with laboratory rats, a rat was thrown into a tank of water; it struggled and thrashed around, swimming for almost sixty hours before it finally drowned. A second rat was held in the experimenter's hand for a few minutes; the experimenter curled his fingers tightly around the rat as if to strangle or suffocate it. The rat struggled against the experimenter for several minutes before finally going limp. The rat was then thrown into the same tank of water; it struggled for less than two minutes before sinking to the bottom and dying.

Why was there such a difference in the reaction between the two rats once they hit the water?

The second rat had already given up hope of survival. It was suffering from the stress that accompanies *hopelessness*, and that stress rendered it incapable of fighting for its life.

The same applies to human beings: Those who have "given up" or who determine that they are in a helpless or hopeless situation undergo actual physical changes that can lead to death. Sudden death can also occur in those who struggle incessantly (in a job, family situation, or social context) without experiencing satisfaction or success.[24]

In 1965, George L. Engel did a study in which he located 275 newspaper clippings that documented cases of sudden death. A follow-up of these cases showed that certain events preceded the deaths. Engel was able to categorize these events in the following groups:

1. A traumatic event involving a close human relationship
2. A situation that involved danger, struggle, or attack (none of which directly caused the fatality)
3. A loss of status or an episode causing humiliation or defeat
4. A situation involving great triumph or personal joy

Engel concluded: "The victims are confronted with events that are impossible to ignore either because of their abrupt, unexpected, or dramatic quality or because of their intensity, irreversibility, or persistence." This perpetuates the idea that feelings of helplessness and hopelessness may play a part in sudden death from stressful situations.[25]

Prediction of death. People under stress who decide that they are going to die—such as patients who face a surgical operation—often experience a predilection for death: They predict their own deaths. For some who are burdened with excessive stress, death is viewed as a welcome escape from problems and pain; death actually may occur within an extremely brief period of time.

Life changes. Stress-provoking life changes (as listed in the Evaluation of Stressful Events on page 24), such as death of a spouse, marriage, divorce, foreclosure of a mortgage, or loss of a job, can result in sudden death due to the body's inability to accommodate the changes that occur in the cardiovascular system. As discussed earlier, stress causes physiological changes, among them a pounding of the heart, rapid circulation of the blood, and constriction of the arteries and vessels leading to skeletal muscles. When the body cannot tolerate these reactions to severe stress, heart attack results, and sudden death is the end result of the stress situation.

Hypertension.   High blood pressure is a well-documented effect of prolonged and severe stress, and can also occur after a brief period of
intense or unexpected stress. If it is severe enough, hypertension due to
stress can result in death.

Cardiac rhythms.   Because stress clearly affects the heart's rhythm,
cardiac arrhythmias that accompany sudden and long-term intensified
stress can cause sudden death.

Myocardial necrosis.   Long-term stress that cannot be resolved by the
physical systems of the body results in chemical secretions that actually
cause deterioration of the heart muscle, leading to sudden and unexpected death.

Arteriosclerosis.   Disease and damage involving the coronary arteries is a
common result of prolonged or intense stress, and can result in myocardial infarction, leading to sudden death.

The dive reflex.   A reflex occurs when you dive into a pool full of water:
The heart slows down, blood flow to the skin and internal organs is
reduced, arterial blood pressure is increased, blood pH is reduced, lactic
acid is increased, carbon dioxide in the blood increases, and potassium
levels in the blood increase. This reflex can also occur as a result of
severe stress (either long-term or sudden). If these physiological
changes are not promptly corrected—as they are when a diver returns
to the surface of the water—sudden death can result.

IMMUNITY TO DISEASE

Because they alter the functioning of the body's immunologic system as
a result of their effects on the central nervous system, stress and
distress impair the body's ability to resist disease.[26]
    Disease is a result of several factors working together: the pres-
ence of bacteria, a virus, or some other disease-causing element; host
tissue in the body that can be affected by the disease-causing element
(such as lungs that can be inflamed by tuberculosis bacteria); and some
internal or external factor that lowers the body's resistance to the
disease-causing factor. Stress—particularly stress severe enough to

result in depression—can lower the body's ability to resist disease and infection. This decreased immunity can make the body susceptible to communicable diseases of all kinds and to certain other diseases such as heart disease, cancer, and respiratory illness.

Heart Disease

A number of risk factors lead to the development of heart disease;[27] among them are cigarette smoking, high blood cholesterol levels, obesity, lack of exercise, diabetes, family history and genetic makeup, and age. But physical factors alone will not determine that a person will develop heart disease or will die from a heart attack: The determining factor is the individual's ability to cope with stress.

The prime candidates for heart attack and heart disease are the Type A personalities—people who are highly competitive, who feel pressured for time, who set deadlines and quotas for themselves, who feel frustrated when they can't meet their impossibly high goals, and who react to frustration with hostility. Type A people are prime candidates because they create stress for themselves and because their high levels of stress interfere with their bodies' ability to return to a normal state of affairs.

Other causes of heart disease and heart attack are the stresses that accompany life changes such as deep personal loss, change in environment, move to a new community, or demotion in a job.

Stress causes the following physical changes, all of which can lead to heart disease and heart attack:

1. Cholesterol levels in the bloodstream are increased; these cholesterol deposits adhere to the walls of the arteries, causing a narrowing and hardening of the arteries.
2. Blood is sent coursing through the arteries at a high pressure, causing hypertension and high blood pressure.
3. Fatty deposits formed from cholesterol and plaque break away from the artery walls, traveling through the bloodstream and lodging in the heart, lung, or brain, causing death. The deposits tear away in response to stress and its effect on the pressure of the bloodstream.
4. Physiological changes that occur as a result of stress increase the body's blood-clotting mechanism, causing the blood to thicken and clot in the arteries, which can lead to death.

Respiratory Illness

The greater the intensity of stress, the greater the likelihood that disease will develop, and the greater the likelihood that the disease will be serious enough to cripple or kill. Respiratory illnesses[28]—especially tuberculosis, asthma, sore throat, the common cold, and hay fever—have been positively linked to stress and its effects on the body.

Three kinds of stress seem to precipitate respiratory illness:

1. Failure and disappointment (which lead to a sense of personal helplessness and hopelessness)
2. Separation from family and friends or a modification in the relationship to family and friends
3. Rising status and positive achievement

People suffering from depression that overwhelms or frightens them are especially high-risk in relation to respiratory illness. With such stress-invoked depression, four factors seem to cause serious respiratory illness:

1. A sense of impending failure or an actual failure in an aspect of life that is important to the individual. (For instance, a woman who prides herself on being a good mother may develop an acute case of asthma serious enough to require hospitalization if her neglect results in her child being struck and killed by an automobile.)
2. A sense of helplessness to change what happens as a result of the failure. (The mother whose child has been killed by a car, for example, cannot restore life to the child, nor can she reverse the chain of events that led to the child's death.)
3. The feeling that one is responsible for the failure. (The mother whose child is killed by a car may decide that she is to blame because she left the child in the care of another child who was too young while she went into town to run errands. She feels guilty that she did not take the child with her or leave the child under adult supervision.)
4. A sense of being isolated and without support. (The mother whose child was killed by an automobile may feel an overwhelming sense of grief and may decide that others around her—her husband, her young children, the neighbors—can't really understand what she is going through because none of them is a mother who has lost a child in such a tragic manner.)

The more severe and intense the stress invoked by the sense of failure and helplessness, the more severe the disease that results and the greater the likelihood of death.

Cancer

Although they do not yet understand the exact physiological reasons, medical researchers recently concluded that stress is a definite cause of cancer;[29] the most probable explanation is the tendency of stress to reduce the body's ability to fight disease in general.

In 1976, Bernard H. Fox hypothesized that stress may be a factor in causing cancer because stress results in a lowered resistance of the body to cancer cells. Fox definitely feels that environmental stressors can depress the immune response.[30]

As with other illnesses and diseases, certain kinds of stress seem to precipitate cancer. Among these are severe depression resulting from stress, a sense of hopelessness, and deep personal loss.

Lawrence LeShan observed this phenomenon and found that in the cancer patients he studied, three out of four of the patients had feelings of "bleak hopelessness about ever achieving any real feelings or meaning or enjoyment in life."[31] He found that these patients believed that all their efforts in life would ultimately fail, which produced intense feelings of despair. Typically, these cancer patients were isolated as children. They did enjoy a full life and satisfaction as young adults, but later on in life they experienced a significant loss. It was after this loss and its resulting hopeless feelings that the cancer developed in these patients.

In addition, researchers have discovered that there is a distinct "cancer personality" which, like that of the person prone to heart disease, is that of a Type A person. Basic to this personality is the overriding stress and anxiety that lead to depression. Many cancer victims also have spells of confusion, disorientation, and phobia.

Of special interest was a recent study of women who developed cancer of the breast or cervix. Those developing cancer of the breast commonly suffered from depression and guilt; they had a disturbance in their identification as women and had a history of excessive responsibility during childhood. Women who develop breast cancer tend to have increased oral-dependent sexual needs and suffer from a disturbance of the heterosexual impulses. The breast cancer is, in effect, a passive way of committing suicide.

Common to women who develop cancer of the cervix is a disturbance over sexual activities and a guilt related to sexual performance or activity.

Other Diseases

A number of other diseases are related directly to the amount of stress created by lifestyle. Ulcers—both gastric and duodenal—have long been identified with stress and anxiety, and are a result of the physiological changes created in the body in response to stress, including the excretion of excess digestive acids and the secretion of hormones that lead to tissue destruction. Migraine headache, tension headache, colitis, loss of teeth (due to grinding and chemical damage to the gums), gum disease, growth of extra teeth, chronic low back pain, and a number of childhood diseases are all attributed to stress and to the body's inability to cope with stress by returning its systems to normal.

PSYCHOSOMATIC ILLNESS AND HYPOCHONDRIA

You've probably heard the terms *psychosomatic illness* and *hypochondria*, and you may have confused the two: Stan's ulcer is actually a psychosomatic illness, the doctor said, and Maren's ulcer is due to the fact that she is a hypochondriac. So Stan's illness and Maren's illness are actually the same, right?

Wrong.

We are made up of two components: a physical body and a mind (or spirit). Many people regard the two to be one unit, in which things that affect one part of the unit affect the unit in its entirety; others deal with the mind and the body as separate entities requiring separate treatment and consideration.

Whether you consider the mind and body to be separate or united, you should realize that the mind has powerful effects on the body.

The body cannot be cured without the mind.

Hippocrates

Stress, in fact, is a product of the mind working on the body—it's a process where the mind prompts the body to become prepared for an emergency or a situation requiring excess strength and action.

Psychosomatic is a term derived from the words *psyche*, meaning mind, and *soma*, meaning body. A psychosomatic disease, then, is a disease that results from the mind's influence over the body. A psychosomatic disease is *caused* by the mind, but the symptoms are very real. A psychosomatically induced ulcer, for instance, is an actual open sore in the stomach lining; a psychosomatically induced heart attack involves actual tissue destruction to the heart and irregularity in the heart's rhythm—it can even cause death.

A *hypochondriac*, on the other hand, *thinks* he or she is ill. But this is not true. The hypochondriac has an excessive preoccupation with supposed ill health. He or she may experience extreme discomfort after eating, may suffer from heartburn, and may have sharp pains in the abdomen—all the classic symptoms of ulcer. Upon examination, however, even a test including X-ray examinations, the patient's stomach is verified to be completely normal. A hypochondriac may suffer all the symptoms of any one of a hundred diseases, although the symptoms rarely fit any acceptable medical pattern. But laboratory tests will always come back negative.

That's where the difference lies: The hypochondriac's illness is all in his or her head, while the psychosomatic illness is simply *caused* by the head. A hypochondriac's stomach lining is healthy and unmarred; a patient with a psychosomatically induced ulcer has an ulcerated stomach lining that is aggravated by excess stomach acid and that may even bleed.

As mentioned earlier in this chapter, doctors now believe that all illnesses may be caused in part by stress—by the way we react to stressors in our environment. So all diseases and illnesses might be considered, at least partially, as psychosomatically induced. But that's a far cry from considering all of us to be hypochondriacs!

COPING WITH STRESS

We all have some stress in our lives—it's unavoidable in our present-day society. And we all cope with it in different ways and with different degrees of success.

EVALUATION OF COPING ABILITY

To find out how well you cope with stress, answer yes or no to each of the following questions:

Do you have a continuous feeling of anxiety?

Does your anxiety sometimes develop into panic?

Are you tired most of the time?

Does it seem as if you are unable to get enough sleep, no matter how early you go to bed or how late you sleep?

Do you worry about your health constantly?

Does your work or your personal life suffer because of the worry that you have about your health?

Do you often feel depressed for no good reason?

Is it hard for you to relax?

Are you plagued by "the shakes" (sudden tremors)?

Is it frightening for you to be alone?

Do you ever just want to "end it all"?

Do you sometimes wonder if you are losing your mind?

When someone else criticizes you, do you interpret it as a personal threat or as a rejection?

Do you lose your temper often?

Is it hard for you to get along with people?

Is it hard for you to concentrate?

Do you feel remote or separated from things that you used to feel close to, including people (family or friends), sports, or books?

Have you become careless about your appearance and cleanliness?

Do you worry a lot?

Do you take life pretty seriously, and, therefore, enjoy it less than you used to?

Do you need tranquilizers in order to make it through the day?

Is it hard for you to make small decisions, such as what to have for dinner or what clothing to wear for the day?

Do you dread ordinary everyday situations, such as going to the grocery store or caring for your children?

Has your attitude toward food changed?

Do you find that you live in the past?

Scoring: If you answered yes to five of the questions, you are not coping as well as you should, and you may be heading for trouble. If you answered yes to eight or more questions, you should seek help from a doctor, minister, or mental health clinic in coping with the stressful situations indicated.

If you're determined to change your coping abilities, there *are* things you can do. There are ways you can boost your coping ability that will guarantee success in dealing with stressful situations in your own life.

Some people choose simply not to cope. There are all kinds of approaches: the ostrich, who refuses to see the existence of a problem; the chicken, who sees the problem but runs away from it; the bulldog, who sees the problem and sticks around but doesn't deal with the problem; and the ant, who sees the problem, confronts the stress, assumes responsibility for the stress, and works, bit by bit, to remove or overcome it.

If you're determined to take the "ant approach" and cope well with the stress in your life, try some of the following suggestions:

1. Learn to relax. The actual method of relaxation depends on what works best for you. Some things that may be very relaxing to one person may actually induce additional stress in another. Assess ways in which you can relax during the day; try taking a short nap in the afternoon, taking a fifteen-minute walk during the morning break at work, finding a quiet place to be by yourself during the day, taking a hot bath when you get home from work, massaging your feet, reading a favorite book or magazine, or taking up a hobby (such as carpentry, sewing, quilting, writing, or hiking). The important thing is to regularly spend time doing something that you enjoy and at which you do not feel pressure to succeed. You should learn to take time out of your schedule to simply sit back and take a breather—to forget about the problems that are weighing on you as a result of your job, your family, or some social situation that concerns you.

Don't choose something that you think will be good for you as a leisure-time activity: Choose something that you *like*. Really enjoy yourself.

Relaxation techniques such as yoga and meditation work well for some people; get a good book that describes the technique and practice it with a few friends who are interested in relaxing, too!

2. Get enough exercise. Exercise has all kinds of benefits; one of them is that it provides a physical release for the pent-up rage and hostility that accompany stress. The better physical shape you're in, the better you will handle stress, and the less likely you will be to follow a chronic stress pattern. Exercise produces biochemical changes, and it provides one way to help your body return to normal by working off the chemicals and changes resulting from stress.

In addition, exercise can help you relax by lessening the tension placed on muscles and body organs. It helps increase circulation, contributing to a sense of overall well-being, and helps develop self-confidence and a sense of accomplishment. Before beginning any exercise program, check with your doctor for suggestions as to which exercises will best benefit you in consideration of your total general fitness, your body type, any physical disabilities you may have, and your body's tolerance level.

One final important consideration: You should *like* the exercise you're doing. Try playing racquetball with your best friend, swimming, playing tennis with your husband, jogging with a group from the office, or playing basketball on the church team. Whatever kind of exercise you choose, it should provide a chance to relieve your boredom, excite your senses, and provide relaxation and fun.

3. Organize your day according to what you really want to do. This means taking a realistic look at yourself, your capabilities, and your goals. For a few days, try making a list of things that you need or want to do. Look at the list, and decide which things on it are absolutely crucial—eating lunch, for example—and which things you can delegate to someone else—for instance, meeting with a stubborn client about an account that you share with several other executives. Decide which things on the list will help you reach your goals for the day, the week, or the year, and which aren't really important. Then concentrate on the things that are necessary, that you enjoy, and that will help you achieve your goals. It is important to feel a sense of satisfaction and accomplishment, so keep your list within the bounds of what you can realistically handle: Overshooting or overestimating your abilities will only lead to frustration and a sense of failure when you are unable to complete everything on your list.

4. Learn to keep crises in their places. Learn to distinguish between minor crises and major ones; you'll find, to your surprise, that most problems and crises in life are minor. When you encounter a minor problem, solve it. Then forget it.

5. Keep an open mind about change. View change as an opportunity to grow and expand as a person.

6. Cancel unnecessary activities out of your life. Learn that life is *not* a constant struggle against the clock.

7. When you feel yourself getting rushed or panicked, stop. Perform some conscious slowdown maneuvers; deep breathing is a good one.

8. Try to work in an environment that is peaceful. If you work in your home, take measures necessary to make your home a happy, relaxing place to live in.

9. Learn to live day by day, instead of always living in the future. Pay attention to what is going on here and now. Look around and try to learn to appreciate the beauty and enjoyment available to you *today* instead of constantly driving yourself for some intangible and vague beauty and enjoyment that you will be able to enjoy only in the future.

10. If something is worrying you, talk it over with a trusted friend or family member.

11. If you encounter a problem, whether serious or mild, escape for a brief time to give yourself a chance to collect your thoughts and calm your emotions. Go to a movie, go for a walk, play with your child, get involved in a basketball game. After a *short* escape, return to your problem and tackle it.

12. When you feel pent-up rage, frustration, or emotion of any kind, do something physically active. Rake the lawn, weed the garden, ride your bicycle to campus and back, have a race with your child to the end of the block, or challenge your best friend to a quick game of tennis.

13. If you are frequently involved in quarrels and if you are usually defiant, learn to give a little. It is important that you hold your ground where principles and moral values are involved, but refusing to budge on a nonessential issue is stupid and serves to increase your stress level.

14. If you are faced with a workload that seems unbearable, divide it into a series of smaller tasks. Then tackle the tasks, *one by one*, until you finish the larger job.

15. Don't try to be perfect in everything you do. You are a human being and, therefore, are subject to frailty and error. You should give everything you do your best effort, but you should not criticize and belittle yourself if your job isn't perfect. If you've done your best, that's all you can possibly be expected to do.

16. Learn to control your competitive nature and avoid irritating, overly competitive people.

17. Get enough sleep. This is critical—sleep helps your body recover from stress by allowing it time to heal and slow down.

18. Learn to concentrate on a task or job while you are doing it. Concentrate on one thing at a time. Fight the tendency to let your mind wander to some other problem or task until you have finished the one you are working on.

19. Concentrate on enriching yourself and developing your aesthetic sense.

20. Learn how to say no to things that you don't want to do.

21. Get up and stretch periodically when you are working.

22. Try some instant relaxers whenever you feel stress coming on: Bend at the waist, letting your arms dangle, and sway slowly from side to side. Drop your chin to your chest and rotate your head slowly in a complete circle. Tilt your head several times to each side in a bouncing motion. Massage your neck (or, better yet, have someone else rub your neck and shoulders). Lie down with your feet elevated for fifteen minutes.

23. Learn—and practice—yoga or some other meditation form.

24. Eat the proper kinds of foods in the proper amounts. People who are under stress have greater nutritional needs than people who are not prone to stress. It is critical that you get enough protein, vitamins, and minerals to repair the tissues that have been damaged as a result of stress. Avoid starchy, sugary food and empty junk-food calories; eat a well-balanced diet that includes meat, dairy foods, fresh fruits, and fresh vegetables as well as whole grains found in breads and cereals. Keep your weight down, too. Excess weight places extra stress on the same body organs and functions that stress does—and it might be the straw that breaks *your* back.

25. Realize and appreciate your own value as a human being with potential and talent.

26. Allow yourself to express your emotions freely within the bounds of appropriateness.

27. If you have difficulty dealing with someone with whom you are forced to interact on a daily or regular basis (such as a close colleague), approach the person in a calm and rational manner and let him or her know what upsets you. Don't use language such as "*You always* chew your pencils" or "*You never* empty the garbage can by the desk." Instead, say something like, "*I* have a hard time concentrating when you chew your pencil," or "It's hard for *me* to remember to empty the garbage can next to the desk every day; can we split the job and each take two days a week?"

28. Hurrying is a learned behavior—it can be changed. Learn to live by the calendar, not by the stopwatch. Slow down; plan far enough ahead so that you aren't always in a rush.

29. Learn to love people around you. Try loving people and using things instead of the other way around.

30. Use quiet, soothing music to help calm yourself down.

31. Take active steps to manage your environment; pinpoint the things in your everyday surroundings that cause you stress, and eliminate or change as many of them as you can.

32. Let people know what they can expect out of you and how much time you are willing to give them.

33. Practice eating more slowly. Learn to savor your food. Put your fork down in between bites; take a sip of water frequently.

34. Once you have mastered the skill of eating slowly, try slowing down in other areas. Walk more slowly; talk more slowly.

35. Plan leisurely, less structured vacations. You will find that a spontaneous vacation can be fun and relatively worry-free.

36. Set your own guidelines and standards for behavior. Quit worrying about what everyone else thinks: If you're happy, that's what is important.

37. Try to be positive in your outlook. It's easy to be critical and to find the negative in people and things. For a week, try to find the *positive* instead.

38. Everyone makes mistakes. Try using yours to your advantage. Instead of dwelling on some bad experience, building up a pressure cooker of guilt and shame, turn the experience around and decide what positive things you can learn from it.

39. Treat those around you with respect.

40. Do what you can to improve relationships that are important to you. It might be a romantic partner, a sister who is attending the same university you are, the grandmother with whom you are living. An important and major source of stress stems from personal relationships—do what you can to make sure yours are working as well as they can. Learn to cultivate quality friendships and relationships.

41. Remember that there are always options and alternatives. All of us make plans, and all of us are disappointed when our plans do not materialize or when things do not go as we would wish them to. It is *not* the end of the world—or even a major crisis—if something doesn't work out for you. Remember, there are *always* options. Take a deep breath, sit down, and figure out a different way of accomplishing your goal or dream. You are in command if you take the time and intelligence to be in command.

42. Get in touch with your needs.

43. Have a good laugh! Researchers now believe that besides being fun, laughing can actually benefit your health, both physically and emotionally.[32] Laughing relieves tension, combats boredom, provides a healthy emotional outlet, and makes life more enjoyable.

The most important keys to managing stress are to involve yourself in activities that you enjoy and to eliminate sources of stress from your life. If your mother wants you to be a veterinarian but you want to be an accountant, choose a college curriculum that will allow you to fulfill your own goal and to do the thing that makes you happiest. If you decide to develop a regular program of exercise, choose activities that are fun for you: jumping rope when it's blizzardy outside, playing tennis when it's warm. If you need a part-time job while you go to school, find something that you enjoy doing—one person might love milking the cows at the university's experimental dairy farm while another might enjoy sitting at a receptionist's desk in the student center. If you experience stress when you are forced to interact with strangers, *don't* accept the receptionist's job no matter how desperate you are for the money. Hold out for something that will allow you to relax—maybe the cows are just for you.

In other words, make good choices for *you*. Don't do something because it's expected, or because everyone else is doing it. Don't buy season tickets to the football games if football bores you; consider tickets to the symphony instead, or spend your Saturday afternoons during the fall semester building a car for your younger brother to race in the soapbox derby.

Take control. Take it easy. And, above all, have fun. Once you have learned to value yourself as a person, you will find it easy to protect yourself from the ravages of diseases that are caused by needless stress.

Notes

[1]Curriculum Concepts, Inc., *Stress!* Chicago: American Hospital Association, 1977, p. 4.

[2]Tom Ferguson. "Stress-Unstress: A Conversation with Ken Pelletier." *Medical Self-Care*, 1978, p. 5

[3]Rosalind Forbes. *Life Stress*. New York: Doubleday, 1979, p. 13.

[4]Donald B. Ardell. *High Level Wellness*. Emmaus, Pa.: Rodale Press, 1977, p. 134; also cited in *Stress Without Distress*. Philadelphia: Lippincott, 1974, p. 111.

[5]Matthew J. Culligan and Keith Sedlacek. *How to Kill Stress Before It Kills You*. New York: Grosset & Dunlap, 1976.

[6]*Feel Younger—Live Longer*. Skokie, Ill.: Rand McNally, 1976, p. 74.

[7]Philip Goldberg. *Executive Health*. New York: McGraw-Hill, 1978, p. 27.

[8]Ardell, p. 134.

[9]Forbes, p. 16.

[10]Daniel A. Girdano and George S. Everly, Jr. *Controlling Stress and Tension: A Holistic Approach*. Englewood Cliffs, N.J.: Prentice-Hall, 1979, p. 68.

[11]Tom Hirsh. "Stress," *National Safety News*, January 1979, p. 38.

[12]*Feel Younger—Live Longer*, p. 80.

[13]Hirsh, p. 34.

[14]Goldberg, 1978, p. 39.

[15]Thomas H. Holmes and Minoru Masuda. " Psychosomatic Syndrome," *Psychology Today*, April 1972.

[16]Ibid.

[17]Howard R. and Martha E. Lewis. *Psychosomatics: How Your Emotions Can Damage Your Health*. New York: Viking, 1972, p. 5.

[18]Holmes and Masuda.

[19]Claude A. Frazier. "The Anxious Mind and Disease," *Nursing Care*, January 1977, p. 17.

[20]W. P. Wilson and B. S. Nashold. "Pain and Emotion," *Postgraduate Medicine*, May 1970, p. 184.

[21]A. Lynn Cope. "Pain: Its Psychological Aspects," *The Journal of Practical Nursing*, January 1977, p. 30.

[22]Cope, p. 31.

[23]Joel E. Dimsdale. "Emotional Causes of Sudden Death," *The American Journal of Psychiatry*, 134, no. 12 (December 1971), p. 1361.

[24]J. G. Bruhn and others. "Psychological Predictors of Sudden Death in Myocardial Infarction," *Journal of Psychosomatic Research*, 18 (1974), pp. 187–191.

[25]Kenneth R. Pelletier. *Holistic Medicine: From Stress to Optimum Health*. New York: Delacourt Press, 1979, p. 103.

[26]George F. Soloman. "Emotions, Stress, the Central Nervous System, and Immunity," *Annals of the New York Academy of Sciences* (1979), pp. 335–342; George L. Engel. "The

Psychosomatic Approach to Individual Susceptibility to Disease," *Gastroenterology* 67 (1974), pp. 1085–1093.

[27]David C. Glass. "Stress, Competition, and Heart Attacks," *Psychology Today*, December 1976, pp. 55–57.

[28]Martin A. Jacobs, Aron Z. Spilken, Martin M. Norman, and Luleen S. Anderson. "Life Stress and Respiratory Illness," *Psychosomatic Medicine*, 32, no. 3 (May–June 1970), pp. 233–242; Aman U. Khan. "Present Status of Psychosomatic Aspects of Asthma," *Psychosomatics*, July–August 1973, pp. 195–200; Thomas J. Luparello. "When Emotional Conflict Complicates Respiratory Disease," *Medical Insight*, April 1971, pp. 22–35.

[29]Frida G. Surawicz, Dennis R. Brightwell, William D. Weitzel, and Ekkehard Othmer. "Cancer, Emotions, and Mental Illness: The Present State of Understanding," *American Journal of Psychiatry*, 133 (November 1976), pp. 1306–1309.

[30]Pelletier, p. 114.

[31]Lewis and Lewis, pp. 272–273.

[32]Farrell and Wilbur Cross. "Cheers! A Belly Laugh Can Help You Stay Well," *Sci/Di*, November 1977, p. 16.

chapter three
DEPRESSION

Everyone experiences stress at some time and to some degree.

Everyone, too, experiences depression.

For most of us, depression is temporary and fleeting; it comes as a reaction to loss or difficulty and is resolved as we work to overcome problems.

Sometimes, and for some people, depression becomes so deep and overwhelming that it interferes with the ability to function. The lifestyle is disturbed, and illness may occur. When we are no longer able to overcome depression, when it begins to interfere seriously, professional help should be sought.

Depression, the blues, depressive illness—whatever you choose to call it—is one of the most common and oldest of all medical disorders. Descriptions of this disease are found sprinkled throughout literary history, including the Bible. Today in the United States alone, 125,000 people are hospitalized yearly for depressive symptoms and over 200,000 receive outpatient treatment.[1] And these figures represent only a fraction of the number of persons who suffer from some form of depressive illness without receiving medical attention. Nearly everyone, at one time or another, has slipped over the edge of temporary sadness into depression.

By definition, depressive illness refers to a grouping of emotional disorders which range from temporary periods of mild dejection to incapacitating illnesses that may result in suicide.

Depression is an emotional reaction, characterized by feelings of sadness, loneliness, rejection, failure, or hopelessness, or a combination of them. It is regarded as indicative of mental illness when it is out of proportion to the circumstances or when it persists beyond a reasonable time and the subject makes no effort to rouse himself from the state or to cope with the circumstances that generated it.[2]

James A. Brussel and Theodore Irwin

Depression is a normal and natural emotion. In fact, we would be abnormal if we could not suffer from this emotion in the form of grief during very stressful periods of life, such as death in the family, loss of employment, or other real or imagined loss. Anyone can become depressed under conditions of sufficient strain.

Most of us recover quickly from these temporary states of sadness. However, there seem to be a significant number of people who are excessively vulnerable to stress. About 15 percent of adult Americans between the ages of eighteen and seventy-four may suffer from the disease known as clinical depression.[3]

These persons respond to their environment in such a way that their depression becomes serious and chronic. As a result, they may have psychic, emotional, and physical symptoms that are very real. These symptoms may become so serious that they handicap the persons, or the symptoms may even prove to be fatal.

Depression is probably an underlying factor in a large portion of physical illnesses. It is also a common denominator in drug addiction, alcoholism, suicide, and other states of social deviance such as homosexuality. Thus it can be considered a major health concern for all society.

Depression occurs more often in middle or old age than in the young. About 8 percent of men and 16 percent of women can expect to suffer from a depressive illness during their lifetime.[4] It is estimated that four to eight million Americans need treatment for depressive illnesses each year, although only a few receive actual treatment.[5]

Major depression is a recurrent illness. If you have a period of major depression, the chance of a recurrence at some time in your life is 80 percent.[6]

The average length of an untreated attack of depression is about six months.

The national cost of depressive disorders in terms of treatment expenses and reduced productivity is estimated at between $1.3 billion and $4.0 billion each year.[7] Also to be considered is the waste in lives from disability, unhappiness, withdrawal from personal and social activities, and suicide. Depression that is not diagnosed and treated can hinder recovery from physical illness.

> Depression is an emotional state of dejection and sadness, ranging from mild discouragement and downheartedness to feelings of utter hopelessness and despair.
>
> National Association for Mental Health

CLASSIFICATION OF DEPRESSIONS

There seem to be as many systems for classifying depression as there are cases. Depression may be a long-term problem with periodic recurrences, a problem that arises in the middle of other psychiatric disorders, or a singular, somewhat isolated, event. It can even be regarded in some cases as a normal reaction to stress and not a disorder.

Everyone is familiar with the low, sad, down-in-the-dumps feelings which occasionally hit for no apparent reason. These feelings are usually transient and quickly self-limiting. The "blues" include the normal variations in moods we experience during the day or week.

Depression can become more pronounced than the blues, and this profound depression can result from either environmental factors or factors found within the individual.

Depression caused by environmental factors usually takes the form of a loss. It is triggered by a situation such as job loss, death, divorce, threats to sexual identity, damage to the social status, physical illness, a geographic move, or failure of children. The instant, temporary reaction to these losses usually is grief, which is a normal and healthy phenomenon—if it is not carried to extremes.

Depression caused by external factors is generally the most common type. It usually doesn't require professional counseling or drug treatment. Emotional support will probably be necessary, however, until the loss has been worked through and resolved. In such cases, reassurance is more important than medication. If this loss is accompanied by lingering guilt or a sense of inadequacy, professional help may be necessary.

Other, more serious types of depression come from within the individual. They are not necessarily an inherited condition, but they can be caused by a deep-seated problem that may date back to childhood. It is typical for someone with this type of depression to dwell upon his or her unhappy experiences in life such as injury, neglect, defeat, and failure. Professional counseling is often required.

> A third of a physician's office practice is almost entirely physical, a third almost entirely psychological, and the middle third a mixture of the physical and psychological. Of the latter two-thirds, I would wager that most of these patients are depressed.
>
> Anonymous physician

SIGNS AND SYMPTOMS OF DEPRESSION

Did you ever wonder whether you might suffer from depression?

Depression can stem from a number of sources and can be attributed to any of a wide variety of causes. Regardless of what triggered the depression, though, all kinds of depression have four characteristics in common that result in the following four traits.

Specific mood changes.   These mood changes can range from mild sadness to intense, distressing misery—usually accompanied by feelings of hopelessness, despair, and loneliness. These symptoms can be extremely crippling. They can disturb any organ system in the body, contributing to overall misery. The mood changes may be so severe that the person may wish to die, and may even contemplate suicide. The person usually feels worse in the early morning, and improves toward evening (in cases of anxiety, this may reverse).

Change in activity level and level of thinking.   This includes agitation, the inability to concentrate or make decisions, and a slowdown of the thought process in general.

Negative self-concept.   This includes feelings of self-blame, self-reproach, and failure; the person often desires to be punished.

Loss of interest. This may occur in work and home life and relationships, accompanied by a lack of energy and the need to escape and hide.

Table 1 (page 64) summarizes symptoms that generally accompany depresssion.

DURATION AND DEGREE

It's possible to recognize the symptoms of depression, but it takes a professional to determine where unhappiness or so-called normal depression takes off and depressive illness begins.

The key in diagnosing depression seems to be in the duration rather than the degree of the illness. Many depressed people reveal that the major differences aren't in the depth of their sad feelings, but in the extent of their feeling of helplessness and self-blame, their inability to think clearly, and the disruption of their everyday functioning.[8]

> When the Monday morning blahs are still around on Friday, or the weekend slump continues through the following week, it's time to suspect something more serious.
>
> Aaron T. Beck

DISTINGUISHING
DEPRESSION FROM ANXIETY

Anxiety often accompanies depression and may also require active treatment. Anxiety can precipitate depression and even suicide.[9]

In some instances, it is difficult to distinguish between depression and anxiety. The two are frequently present in the same patient. A series of comparative observations are helpful in distinguishing between them.

The depressed patient is most frequently slowed down in such behavior as talk and movement, while the anxious patient most frequently responds normally or is somewhat speeded up.

The depressed patient is generally reluctant to discuss his or her social or emotional difficulties, physical symptoms, and the like, or

DEPRESSION SCALE

Depression can be rated on the basis of fifteen statements most frequently made by people with masked depression. Each of the fifteen statements is accompanied by two other statements, one commonly made by overt depressives and another common to mentally healthy persons. The letters o, c, and h have been added to identify overt, covert, and healthy statements; the depressive characteristics for each group appear in parentheses. To find out where you fit in, read each statement; underline those that apply to you. If you are unsure which statement to mark, underline the one that reflects the way you feel most of the time. The statements you underline should give an indication of the way you react to your environment most of the time, not merely during isolated moments of sadness.

1. (motor retardation)
   (O) Everything is an effort.
   (H) I have a lot of energy.
   (C) Maybe I'm just getting older.

2. (anergia)
   (H) I've got a lot of pep.
   (C) I tire easily.
   (O) I'm tired all the time.

3. (dissatisfaction, emptiness)
   (C) I'm in a rut.
   (O) Things are not going well.
   (H) I'm pleased with the way things are going.

4. (pessimism, hopelessness)
   (O) I don't have much to look forward to.
   (H) I look forward to the future.
   (C) I go along as best I can.

5. (diurnal variation)
   (H) I enjoy getting up in the morning.
   (C) I push myself to get going in the morning.
   (O) I find it hard to face the day.

6. (sleep disturbance)
   (C) I don't feel rested after sleeping.
   (O) I've been having trouble sleeping lately.
   (H) I sleep fine and feel rested.

norexia)
  (O) I haven't been eating as well lately.
  (H) I enjoy eating.
  (C) Food doesn't taste as good as it used to.

8. (decreased libido)
  (H) Sex is pleasurable to me.
  (C) Sometimes I'm too tired for sex.
  (O) I have lost some interest in sex lately.

9. (loss of ambition and initiative, apathy)
  (C) I force myself to do my work.
  (O) I don't have much ambition.
  (H) I am ambitious.

10. (disinterest, anhedonia)
  (O) I don't feel like doing much lately.
  (H) I enjoy doing lots of things.
  (C) I don't go out much because I'm too tired.

11. (helplessness, confusion)
  (H) Things are going well.
  (C) Sometimes everything goes wrong.
  (O) I can't cope with things very well lately.

12. (uselessness, worthlessness)
  (C) I'd do better if I felt better.
  (O) Sometimes I can't do anything right.
  (H) Things are running smoothly.

13. (despairing mood, sadness)
  (O) I'm depressed.
  (H) I'm happy.
  (C) I don't let myself get depressed.

14. (guilt and hostility, loss of self-esteem)
  (H) I'm happy with the way I am doing things.
  (C) Everybody feels they could do better.
  (O) I'm not doing things as well as I used to.

15. (despondency, possible suicidal thoughts)
  (O) Sometimes I feel like giving up.
  (H) I'm enjoying my life.
  (C) I fight it when I feel discouraged.

Scoring: Now take a look at the statements you have underlined; for each c and o statement, read the depressive characteristics. Keep those in mind as you identify certain symptoms that are basically characteristic of all kinds of depression.

TABLE 1. General Symptoms of Depression

Physiological Symptoms	Emotional Symptoms	Psychic Symptoms	Behavioral Symptoms
Chronic fatigue	Sadness, the blues	Inability to concentrate	Loss of function
Inability to sleep	Crying	Loss in interest in family events	Withdrawal from activity
Early awakening	Lack of feeling	Poor memory	Psychomotor retardation
Headaches	Apathy toward social life or hobbies	Suicidal thoughts	Lack of attention to grooming routines
Loss of appetite	Anxiety	Lack of enjoyment	Behavior excesses
Weakness and fatigue	Feelings of failure	Failure to feel rested after sleep	Initiation of fewer interpersonal behaviors
Loss of sex drive	Delusions of guilt, self-reproach		Focusing of behavior toward one person
Menstrual changes	Fears of physical illness		
Nausea	Chronic unhappiness		
Sudden weight loss (or gain)	Loss of self-esteem		
Dizzy spells	Irritability, hostility		
Gastrointestinal upsets	Fears of various kinds: of insanity, loneliness, changing jobs, moving		
Dryness in the mouth			
Indigestion			
Constipation			
Dyspepsia			
Heart palpitations			
Slowing speech and movements			

discusses them in a monotone. Discussion of problems generally does not lead to rapid improvement or changes in behavior. The anxious patient, on the other hand, is more likely to discuss his or her symptoms easily or eagerly, to be more animated, and to talk about a variety of topics. Discussing problems will frequently lead to some rapid improvement or changes in behavior.

The depressed patient has markedly decreased interests while the anxious patient generally retains an interest in some things.

The depressed person has real difficulty in enjoying anything, while the anxious person more frequently can enjoy some activities, such as watching TV or talking with others.

The depressed person usually has a decreased appetite, a decreased enjoyment of food, or a weight loss. The anxious person generally has no weight loss (except for patients with anorexia nervosa, a relatively rare condition), may eat constantly or intermittently, and generally enjoys at least some foods.

The depressed person is generally constipated, while the anxious one more frequently has diarrhea or some loosening of bowel movements.

Depression is generally helped by antidepressants and worsened by tranquilizers, while the reverse is true for anxiety. If anxious people pace, they walk a given route repeatedly. Their thoughts center on certain troubling ideas and rarely vary. They repeat the same facts or complaints over and over. Their movements (such as hand motions) tend to be highly repetitive.

The highly anxious patient, without depression, tends to talk rapidly, with variable vocal tone, about many different things. His or her motor behavior tends to be much more variable than that of the depressed patient and has a random, unpredictable nature. See Table 2 for a more detailed description of depression vs. anxiety.[10]

FACTORS RELATED
TO THE ONSET OF DEPRESSION

When is sadness temporary? When can you still cope with loss and disappointment? When are things starting to get out of hand?

They aren't easy questions, and the answers aren't easy, either.

TABLE 2. Common Symptoms of Anxiety, Depression, and Organic Disease

Somatic Symptoms	Anxiety	Depression	Organic Disease
Abdominal pain	common	common	common
Black vomited material	uncommon	uncommon	common
Bloody vomited material	uncommon	uncommon	common
Constipation	common	common	common
Diarrhea	common	uncommon	common
Difficulty breathing	common	uncommon	common
Difficulty concentrating	common	common	common
Fatigue	common	common	common
Inability to breathe except when standing	uncommon	uncommon	common
Indigestion	common	common	common
Insomnia	common	common	common
Lack of appetite	common	common	common
Lack of menstrual period	common	common	common
Lethargy	uncommon	common	common
Loss of libido	uncommon	common	uncommon
Nausea	common	common	common
Numbness or prickling sensations	common	uncommon	common
Productive coughing	uncommon	uncommon	common
Sexual nonresponsiveness	uncommon	common	uncommon
Uninterrupted but unrefreshing sleep	common	common	common
Vomiting	common	common	common

Psychological Findings	Anxiety	Depression	Organic Disease
Alcoholism	common	common	uncommon
Anger	common	common	common
Apathy	uncommon	common	common
Bitterness	common	common	uncommon
Desire for suicide	uncommon	common	uncommon
Evasiveness	common	uncommon	uncommon
Generalized apprehensiveness	common	uncommon	uncommon

Psychological Findings	Anxiety	Depression	Organic Disease
Gloominess	uncommon	common	uncommon
Guilt	uncommon	common	uncommon
Hopelessness	uncommon	common	uncommon
Humorlessness	common	common	uncommon
Hypochondriasis	common	common	uncommon
Irritability	common	common	common
Lack of spontaneity	uncommon	common	common
Loneliness	uncommon	common	uncommon
Long silences	uncommon	common	common
Loss of interest	uncommon	common	uncommon
Nervousness	common	uncommon	common
Panic	common	uncommon	uncommon
Self-blame	uncommon	common	uncommon
Self-deprecation	common	common	uncommon
Sense of personal worthlessness	uncommon	common	uncommon
Tearfulness	uncommon	common	uncommon
Tension	common	uncommon	uncommon
Uncertainty	common	common	uncommon

Physical Findings	Anxiety	Depression	Organic Disease
Confusion	uncommon	common	common
Cool, moist extremities	common	uncommon	common
Diminished breath sounds	uncommon	uncommon	common
Excessive sweating	common	uncommon	common
Flushing	common	uncommon	common
Noisy breathing	uncommon	uncommon	common
Psychomotor retardation	uncommon	common	common
Rapid heart rate	common	uncommon	common
Tremor	common	uncommon	common
Weight loss	common	common	common
Wheezing	uncommon	uncommon	common

You can tell plenty about your depression, though, if you can identify what started it in the first place. Researchers have discovered that some personality types are more prone to depression and that the onset of depression is triggered much more easily in these types.

Personality is a major influence in the depression cycle. But other factors cause depression to escalate to a chronic and serious condition for some people.

Grief reaction.   The triggering mechanism in nearly all cases of depression is psychic pain—some type of loss, disappointment, frustration, or real or imagined threat.

Grief and bereavement are normal and necessary reactions to some of life's stresses such as the loss of a love through death or divorce, loss of limb, or loss of employment.

> In a real dark night of the soul, it is always three o'clock in the morning.
>
> F. Scott Fitzgerald

> Even when Churchill led his country in its most perilous era his rebellion was marked by irritability and impatience. He even denied nature: despite hypertension and countless heart attacks, he ignored his doctor's orders, drank liberally, chain smoked cigars, and slept little. Churchill referred to his depressive attacks as "the black dog" and once remarked that when this mood struck he sometimes wondered whether it would not be better to hurl himself in front of a train and end it all.[11]
>
> James Brussel and Theodore Irwin

Organic factors.   Depression may be associated with organic disorders and diseases such as influenza and infectious hepatitis. Other physical disorders that often accompany depression include anemia, Cushing's syndrome, and arthritis. Depression may follow surgery, particularly mastectomy, prostatectomy, hysterectomy, or surgery on the eyes. Suicide may follow.[12]

Age.   Many young people seem to suffer depression as a result of deliberate alienation from their parents' standards. Their new, self-imposed standards are unreasonable and unreachable. The resulting

DEPRESSION SELF-EVALUATION TEST

Score this test in the following way to find out if you are prone to depression: 1 if the statement is true none or a little of the time; 2 if it is true some of the time; 3 if it is true a good part of the time; and 4 if it is true most of the time.

I want things done my way.
I criticize people who don't live up to my standards or expectations.
I stick to my principles no matter what.
Changes in the environment or the behavior of other people upset me.
I am fussy and meticulous about my possessions.
If I don't finish a task, I get upset.
I insist on full value for everything that I purchase.
I like everything that I do to be perfect.
I follow an exact routine every day.
I do things precisely, down to the last detail.
If my schedule for the day is upset, I get tense and anxious.
I plan ahead so that I won't be late.
When my surroundings are not clean, I get tense and anxious.
I make lists of things I need to do for the day or week.
I worry about minor aches and pains.
I like to be prepared for any emergency that might come up.
I am strict about fulfilling every one of my obligations.
I expect worthy and high moral standards in other people.
When someone takes advantage of me, I get badly shaken.
When people don't replace things exactly as I left them, I get upset.
I keep old things because I think they might be useful someday.
I am sexually inhibited.
I feel better working than relaxing; it is hard for me to take time off.
I am a private person.
I budget myself carefully and live on a cash and carry basis.

Scoring: Add your score. If it is between 25 and 45, you are not compulsive. If it is between 46 and 55, you are mildly obsessive-compulsive, but it works for you instead of against you. You are able to adapt successfully to things that might otherwise upset you. If your score is between 56 and 70, you are moderately obsessive-compulsive: While you are able to adapt to most things, you will have days that are riddled with excessive tension. If your score is between 71 and 100, you are dangerously obsessive-compulsive. You are likely to go through a period of many days marked by high tension, and you need to ease off. The closer your score is to 100, the more likely you are to exhaust your ability to adapt and to slump into a severe depression caused by unrelenting stress.

conflicts plunge them into depression. Higher standards of achievement are expected from greater numbers of young people. We are now
more concerned about college dropouts than dropouts from high
school. Failure in the face of intense competition sparks depression as
does the race for employment, marriage, and unrealistic goals.

Middle age.   During middle age, youth fades and emotional and physical reserves often become more depleted. This, accompanied by
changes in physical attractiveness, job boredom, and rivalry with
younger people, often leads to depression among those with poor
coping skills.

> Why, at the height of success, did William Shakespeare withdraw
> from the theater and retire to Stratford? He had at least a half-a-
> dozen hits running in London, and owned and directed as many
> theaters. The Bard was only forty-eight and it is believed he
> suffered a type of melancholia commonly seen in the middle years.
> Yet when he was only thirty-six Shakespeare was given to morbid
> introspection, as evidenced by his stirring tragedy, *Hamlet* (it was
> Hamlet who fell into "Melancholia" when his father died). . . .
> Morbidness is repeated in Shakespeare's plays again and again—
> *Macbeth, Romeo and Juliet, King Lear*, and many others.[13]
>
>   James Brussel and Theodore Irwin

Depression in the elderly.   Depression in older people is common and is
often incapacitating enough to make treatment difficult. Chronically ill
elderly people are often considered undesirable patients and sometimes
are rejected by our youth-oriented society. Many older depressed patients need frequent short individual sessions to rebuild their self-
esteem. They need time, patience, explanations, and encouragement to
function to the limit of their physical capacity. It is not uncommon for
an elderly patient who has undergone surgery or other extensive
treatment to respond with surprising vigor while recovering in the
hospital, but to slowly become severely depressed once he or she
returns home; this slow progression of depression can lead to an early
death because the person will not eat, loses interest in others, and loses
the desire to live.[14]

Loss of flexibility, depression, dependence, and financial insecurity are precursors to the high rate of suicide in men and women over
sixty.

Loss of reinforcement. For some reason, the depressive individual feels unable to control his or her environment, including interpersonal relationships; environmental stresses then become unmanageable. Although the patient's normal behavior does not provide the success and reinforcement he or she needs, depression results in attention and sympathy, which reinforces this condition.[15]

> Wolfgang Amadeus Mozart died at the early age of thirty-six, but by the time he was thirty he had "written himself out." The first hint of this is his C minor symphony in which, according to musicologists, melancholy had deepened into gloom. Just before he died, Mozart said: "I am at the point of death . . . I thus finish my funeral song. . . ."[16]
>
> James Brussel and Theodore Irwin

Genetic factors. Preliminary studies of individuals with depressive diseases reveal a familial factor. Generally, a parent—often the mother—and other siblings are also afflicted with the condition, which may be sex-linked. More studies are needed in this area.

> If what I feel were equally distributed to the whole human family, there would not be one cheerful face on earth.
>
> Abraham Lincoln

Depression in infants and children. Until recently, it was thought that only adults suffered from depression. However, infants and children are capable of suffering depressive episodes, although the symptoms sometimes vary, depending on developmental stages of growth, from those exhibited in adults. Possible underlying causes of infant and early childhood depression include the following:

Physical defect or illness
Malfunction of endocrine glands
Mental retardation due to brain injury
Brain tumor, abscess, meningitis, or encephalitis
Mismanagement of child in infancy (reflected in developing personality)
Injudicious discipline
Lack of affection that arouses feelings of insecurity
Lack of encouragement for achievements

Failure to gain social acceptance at home or in the "world"

Divorce, desertion, or death of a parent (loss of father before age of sixteen)

Broken home

Parental favoritism toward sibling

Sibling rivalry

Strained relationship between stepparents and stepchild

Strained relationship with foster parents

Economic difficulties

Community antagonism because of ethnic and national differences

Adverse school experiences

Moving to a new home

Punitive measures by playmates, schoolmates, and teachers

Failure in social and occupational milieus

Depression and withdrawal of the mother

The signs and symptoms of depression vary with the child's age: In infancy, the child may simply fail to thrive. A mother who becomes depressed withdraws from her child who, in turn, becomes depressed. The baby will not be able to overcome its depression until the mother overcomes hers; a mother substitute may be required until the mother is fully treated.

Depression in children is often hidden behind a facade of other symptoms and complaints. Among schoolchildren, underlying depression has been implicated in behavior problems, ranging from temper tantrums and truancy to school phobias and academic failure.[17]

Older children may also show depression through abnormal behavior. Angry outbursts, learning difficulties, problems with sleep, and bed-wetting could all represent depressive symptoms. Overeating is a common symptom of depression; other reactions include starvation, seclusion, and hatefulness toward friends or family. Luckily, suicide is not a common way for children to cope with depression.

Unfortunately, a child's emotional problem is often not recognized unless the behavior is actively disturbing or annoying to adults. Passive and withdrawn children are often overlooked. Most children are not fully aware of their own depression and the need to seek direct help.

You might consider depression as a cause if a child continually shows a lack of self-confidence, a low opinion of his or her abilities, feelings of defeat, and a loss of interest in the future. A child might also become difficult to control or hostile, and might change his or her sleeping or eating habits.

Depression in adolescents. Depression in adolescents is common—it usually is a reaction to loss, and adolescents experience many losses in their difficult progress from childhood to adulthood.

Probably the most devastating loss in adolescence is that of self-esteem. Adolescents are especially vulnerable to defeat, and the repeated defeats suffered by an adolescent who has not yet established relationships that would help him or her to tolerate failure often cause depression.

It becomes more difficult to recognize depression in adolescents because the pressures normally accompanying this period of life produce wide behavioral variations. Watch for extended apathy, wide extremes in eating or sleeping, withdrawal from peers, rebellion, running away, defiance, aggression, hostility, narcotic use, compulsive eating, chain smoking, television addiction, or alcoholism.[18] Adolescents particularly prone to depression are those with chronic illnesses such as kidney disease, tuberculosis, or diabetes and those whose parents have chronic marital problems.

Unfortunately, the first obvious sign of severe depression in adolescents may be attempted suicide. When other attempts to deal with feelings fail to bring relief, suicide may appear to be the only way to solve problems or get attention and help.[19]

Postnatal depression. Our society glorifies motherhood; we are taught that it is wonderful to be pregnant, and that the experience of becoming a mother is filled with nothing but joy and satisfaction. More and more people in our country are getting married, and at an earlier age; more and more are giving birth to children as a means of fulfilling the marriage relationship.

Because of these favorable social attitudes, a woman expects to feel marvelous after giving birth to a baby. Many women realize those feelings, but for others, the grief and confusion of postnatal depression become a reality.[20] They feel miserable and unhappy; they experience a letdown, and some even feel as if the whole world has fallen down on top of them. They worry about things that aren't worth worrying about and may burst into tears for no reason at all. Instead of feeling joyful and excited when they look at the baby, they feel frustration. Holding the baby creates tension; feeding the baby and changing diapers become unpleasant tasks. And, to compound the problem, the mother feels guilty about not feeling happy.

There are two different types of postnatal depression, with two different degrees of severity.

The first type occurs immediately after giving birth: The fatigue caused by labor may contribute to the onset of depression. Women who suffer depression at this point are not interested in the child and generally don't want anything to do with it. Sometimes they resent the child; other mothers may even blame the husband. Depression occurring at this stage passes quickly, and generally by the time the mother is ready to leave the hospital and take the baby home, she can scarcely remember a time when she did not cherish the infant.

The second, less common kind of postnatal depression develops at a different time and is much more serious. Once the mother gets the baby home, she becomes hysterical and violent. She totally rejects the child: She not only refuses to cradle and cuddle the infant, but may even refuse to stay in the same room. A woman suffering this kind of depression is dangerous to herself and to her child: She shows absolutely no concern for the child (if the depression becomes severe enough, she may try to kill the baby), and she may become suicidal. Initial treatment consists of sedation until the mother reaches a state of calm, after which more involved therapy must be initiated.

Some mothers suffer a depression immediately after they leave the hospital, but the depression is not violent nor does it pose a particular danger. It is easy to determine the causes for this kind of postnatal depression: When the mother was in the hospital, she had help with the infant. She may have been allowed to bathe, feed, and change the baby, but she was not ultimately responsible for the health and survival of the infant who, of course, was completely dependent on others.

But once the mother gets home, she is often solely responsible for the child. The baby requires a great deal of attention and hard work—if it screams, or if the mother is too tired to cope with its demands, she can't simply ring for a nurse to take over child care duties. And there are other problems. Now that she's back home, she's responsible not only

for the care of the new baby, but for the care and feeding of her husband, other children she may have, and the upkeep of household responsibilities—laundry, cooking, and cleaning. Sometimes it's just too much for her.

In some instances, there's still another pressure. The husband's attitude may change; after the birth of a baby, the relationship between two marriage partners is never quite the same again. It's never just "the two of us" again; some husbands may come to the sudden realization that they no longer command the complete attention of their wives. A woman with a new baby must of necessity spend a great deal of time with the baby, attending to its physical needs. A husband who is used to being the center of his wife's world may not be able to adjust well to what he perceives as "second place," a reaction that certainly places additional stress on the woman.

There are other reasons for this depression: the readjustment of the body following birth, the changing level of hormones, the anxiety over being a good mother, concern over the changing relationship of husband and wife, the fatigue of constant child care, and the alteration of sexual activity for some time following birth.

Luckily, postnatal depression can be dealt with and can be overcome. Try some of these suggestions:[21]

1. Prior to birth, get professional advice about parenthood to help relieve some of the anxieties you are about to face in becoming a parent.
2. Surround yourself with those who have been through the childbirth experience and who can offer you support and help.
3. Continue pursuing your outside interests, but cut down on the amount of responsibility you accept.
4. Arrange for someone to come in and help you with the baby at first.
5. Don't plan to move just before or just after the baby is born.
6. Arrange to attend child care classes at your local hospital; you will learn about labor and delivery, but will also learn about how to care for your baby after you get home.
7. Make sure that your diet is adequate, and especially that it is rich in iron and protein. If you eat properly you will be able to resist the fatigue that so often prolongs and worsens depression.
8. Get plenty of exercise.
9. Even after the baby is born, arrange to spend one evening a week away from the house with your husband, on a "date." Spend the time together

and express your love and concern for each other while you leave the baby with a trusted relative.

10. Take the opportunity to get away from the house periodically so that the stress and pressure of the home do not seem constant. This doesn't have to be a big outing—a trip to the hairdresser, the grocery store, or a friend's house for a brief visit will serve the purpose.

11. Approach any problems openly and honestly. If you coop your feelings up inside, you will only end up hurting yourself. If you have doubts about your ability to care for your child, talk to your doctor, who can help arrange for a class or a nurse to get you through the difficult period. If you are unsure that your husband really wanted the baby, ask him. You can avoid a lot of grief by confronting your feelings and taking care of them.

DEPRESSION AND SUICIDE

Perhaps the most serious problem related to depression is its link to suicidal behavior. Untreated or unsuccessfully treated depression frequently results in suicide. More than 25,000 Americans commit suicide yearly in the United States; the World Health Organization estimates that 1,000 to 2,000 persons in the Western world commit suicide *each day*. Depressive illness has been found to be the cause of up to 80 percent of suicides.[22]

It isn't hard to see why suicidal feelings may arise during depression. The depressive state is an agonizing experience, oftentimes less preferable than physical pain; life may appear meaningless or totally frustrating. It is extremely difficult to convince a depressed person that things will get better, even if he or she has recovered from depression before—depression creates the feeling that one would be better off dead.

> Help Help
> Help I feel life coming closer
> When all I want is to die.
> Marilyn Monroe

Strangely enough, suicide may represent the last attempt of a depressed person to express hope: Suffering reaches the point where the desire for relief outweighs the consideration of negative consequences, the effects on the family, or even the effects on oneself.

Who is likely to try suicide as a result of depression? The person who might be suicidal shows the following signs:[23]

- Looks very sad
- Talks slowly, or only manages to speak with difficulty
- Makes comments about hurting his or her loved ones by staying alive
- Makes many vague statements that reflect deep misery, guilt, or self-deprecation
- Refers subtly or openly to a suicidal intent
- Has a hard time thinking or concentrating
- Is a troubled teenager who has lost a loved one
- Is undergoing puberty
- Is going through menopause
- Is elderly and has lost many of his or her friends and loved ones, has few emotional or financial resources, and is lonely
- Has a chronic illness (especially common among the elderly)
- Has a terminal illness
- Has recently lost a loved one or suffered a blow to his or her self-esteem
- Has had one or more suicides in the family
- Has planned how he or she would commit suicide
- Suffers instability in his or her work or marriage relationship
- Displays self-destructive tendencies (these could include alcoholism, accident-proneness, drunken sprees, constant shifts in employment, or refusal to follow a medical plan or take required medication)
- Withdraws socially
- Seems restless and tense
- Suffered the death of a parent during his or her childhood or before the end of adolescence (loss of a father is particularly significant)

The behavior of a depressed patient can provide clues to suicidal intent. Sudden peacefulness in a severely depressed person may indicate that he or she has decided upon suicide and has found relief from intense pain with the decision. Others anticipating suicide may make out wills, give away valued possessions, ask unusual questions about the lethal doses of drugs, plan to visit a bridge, or make unusual statements such as: "I won't be troubling you anymore."

Every case diagnosed as depression should be considered a suicide risk. The period at the beginning of treatment for depression and the six months following discharge are especially dangerous times. Depression is recurrent and so is the risk of suicide.

The treatment of mental illness such as depression just a few centuries ago dealt not with psychotherapy or drugs, but with such "therapeutic" techniques as exorcism, blood letting, dunkings, floggings and imprisonment. Looking back, it is hard to believe that only 300 years ago, in Europe and Great Britain, stench-filled dungeons served as houses of "correction" for the mentally ill. Victims of emotional disturbances such as depression were likely to be chained in a rat-infested prison.

"Depression: Dark Night of the Soul"

Those who contemplate or threaten suicide walk a fine line and can be swayed either way. If you recognize the symptoms in someone you know, confront that person with your thoughts. Some people mistakenly believe that mentioning suicide to a depressed person may "plant the seed," may inspire the individual to do something he or she hadn't already contemplated. It won't. Instead, a person who is indeed suicidal will feel relieved to have a chance to discuss those feelings openly with someone who wants to listen.

And do take the time to listen. Don't reject the person for having suicidal feelings, and don't try to argue him or her out of it. Don't challenge or dare a person to commit suicide, either. Offer to find help.

The will to live is strong, and if given an audience and the chance for self-expression, the depressed victim will usually start to question his or her reason for wanting to end life. Ventilation of feelings can help lessen the impact of suicidal thoughts and can help the individual regain some objectivity about his or her life.

TREATMENT FOR DEPRESSION

Once depression is diagnosed, it can usually be successfully treated. Good general medical care is basic to any treatment program; underlying medical problems, such as diabetes or high blood pressure, must be dealt with in order to bring depression under control.

There are three basic modes of treatment:

Psychotherapy.   Psychotherapy, which aims at carrying the patient over the depression and changing the personality facets that caused the depression to emerge, is carried out by a psychiatrist or clinical psychologist. Psychotherapy attempts to restore the patient's self-esteem throughout the process of treatment.

Electroshock therapy. Severe forms of depression can often be successfully treated by passing painless electric current through the brain, causing profound alterations in the brain's metabolism. Four to five treatments are usually necessary to ease severe depression.

Drug therapy. The most widespread treatment for depression is the use of mood-altering drugs;[24] biochemical levels are restored to normal, and close supervision by a physician is required. Unlike tranquilizers and amphetamines, antidepressant drugs have little or no effect on people who are not depressed.

A depressed person must realize that he or she is not a victim of the environment, and must learn to master his or her problems. Through proper perspective, meaningful work, participation in pleasant activities, and endurance it is possible to overcome depression.

How to Help

If you know someone who is depressed, there are ways you can help. Try some of the following suggestions:[25]

1. Encourage the individual to have a physical examination by a physician to rule out any organic causes of depression; suggest adequate rest and a balanced diet.
2. If the individual has ceased activities that provide contact with others, suggest participation in such activities.
3. Make sure that the individual is not placed in a situation he or she can't handle; the last thing a depressed person needs is to experience failure.
4. Encourage the person to ventilate and communicate his or her feelings to others.
5. Suggest that the person accompany you on a short vacation.
6. Urge the individual to indulge in something enjoyable such as a new item of clothing, a record, or a dinner at a favorite restaurant.
7. Give the depressed person something else to think about. Plan a lunch at a restaurant, or a shopping trip, suggest a round of golf, or ask for help with simple household chores, such as planting some new shrubs in your front yard.

8. Don't serve the individual alcohol; alcohol only increases depression.

9. Help the person to set a regular schedule of activities that fills each day, so that he or she stays busy and involved.

10. Teach the individual something new—a craft or a skill—that is not too difficult to master. Then provide an opportunity for practice by helping the person make something to give away.

11. Help a depressed person become involved in some kind of physical exercise.

12. Praise the individual genuinely for accomplishments and efforts. Find nice things to say that are honest and sincere.

13. Get the person involved in doing things for others.

14. Help the individual to establish a social support system of people who will provide encouragement and a sense of security. Arrange for a night out with old friends. However, don't insist on a situation that is too festive if he or she doesn't want to participate; this may create more depression for the individual.

15. Help the person to understand his or her limitations without downgrading abilities.

16. Help the individual to establish realistic goals; make sure they are short-term goals that he or she can achieve. The person will experience a sense of renewed self-esteem from the experience of making some kind of progress or achievement.

17. Let the person make decisions in order to feel in control of his or her life. However, don't force a person to make major decisions until you feel that he or she is up to it.

18. Offer support and understanding; a depressed individual doesn't need criticism or rejection. Show that you accept and care for him or her *no matter what.*

You can get further help and advice from any of the following agencies:

American Psychiatric Association
1700 Eighteenth Street, NW
Washington, DC 20009

American Psychological Association
Office of Professional Affairs
1200 Seventeenth Street, NW
Washington, DC 20036

The National Institute of Mental Health
Public Inquiries Branch, Room 11-A-33
5600 Fishers Lane
Rockville, MD 20852

The Mental Health Association
1800 Kent Street
Arlington, VA 22209

PREVENTING DEPRESSION

Little, if anything, has been done in the area of preventing depression. Many psychiatrists feel that people with a predisposition to develop depression may exhibit specific characteristics; if these characteristics could be identified and validated, perhaps special steps could be taken to help these people to improve their mechanisms for dealing with stress before extremely stressful events occur. The biggest problem seems to be in agreeing on the characteristics of those who are prone to depression.

Early diagnosis and effective treatment appear to be the most valuable steps in preventing severe depression at the present time.

Perhaps the only way to avoid depression altogether is not to be born.

"Depression: Dark Night of the Soul"

Notes

[1]James A. Brussel and Theodore Irwin. *Understanding and Overcoming Depression*. New York: Hawthorn Books Inc., 1973, p. 20. Excerpts used by permission of Hawthorn Books, Elsevier-Dutton Publishing Co., Inc.

[2]Ibid.

[3]Ibid.

[4]"Depression: Dark Night of the Soul," West Point, Pa.: Merck Sharp & Dohme, p. 1.

[5]"Depression: Dark Night of the Soul," p. 8.

[6]Brussel and Irwin, pp. 30–31.

[7]Brussel and Irwin, p. 8.

[8]James J. Lynch. *The Broken Heart: The Medical Consequences of Loneliness*, © 1977 by Basic Books, Inc., Publishers, New York, p. 103.

[9]William G. Crary and Gerald C. Crary. "Depression," *American Journal of Nursing*, March 1973, pp. 472–475.

[10]_____ . "Mental Illness—A Course for Primary Care Physicians," *Practical Psychology for Physicians*, February 1977, p. 22.

[11]Brussel and Irwin. *Understanding and Overcoming Depression*, p. 7.

[12]James A. Brussel and Theodore Irwin. "Depression: Psychic Pain as a Cause," *Medical Opinion*, February 1974, pp. 68–76.

[13]Brussel and Irwin. *Understanding and Overcoming Depression*, p. 8.

14"Depression: Masked or Missed?" *Patient Care*, May 1968, pp. 77–121.

15Hagop S. Akiskal and William T. McKinney, Jr. "Depressive Disorders: Toward a Unified Hypothesis," *Science*, 182 (October 5, 1973), pp. 20–29.

16Brussel and Irwin. *Understanding and Overcoming Depression*, p. 9.

17Julius Segal. "Little Boy, Little Girl Blue," *Family Health*, July 1976, p. 39.

18Ghislaine D. Godenne. "The Masked Signs of Adolescent Depression," *Medical Insight*, March 1974, p. 9.

19Norman S. Brandes. "A Discussion of Depression in Children and Adolescents," *Clinical Pediatrics*, 10, no. 8, p. 471.

20David Cohen. "What Is Post-Natal Depression?" *Continuing Education*, December 1976, pps. 19–21.

21Michael Newton. "New Baby! Why So Sad?" *Family Health/Today's Health*, May 1976, pp. 17, 64.

22Virginia Rosslyn. *Depression, The Thin Edge*, Washington, D.C.: National Association for Mental Health, 1973.

23Bernard Bressler. "Depression and Suicide," *Consultant*, March 1978, p. 125.

24"Depression: Masked or Missed?" pp. 77–121.

25List compiled from "Depression: When the Blues Become Serious," *Changing Times*, March 1978, pp. 37–39; Virginia Rosslyn. *Depression: The Thin Edge*, Washington, D.C.: National Association for Mental Health, 1973; Mary L. Smith. "Depression: You See It—But What Do You Do About It?" *Nursing '78*, September 1978, pp. 43–45; Kathleen Earley. "The Constant Sorrow," *The Sciences*, November 1974, pp. 13–17; and John Cohen. "How to Cope with Depression," *Continuing Education*, December 1976, pp. 24–28.

chapter four
HELPING AND UNDERSTANDING PEOPLE IN CRISIS

Most of the time, we are able to handle stress and depression; they may come, and they may persist for a certain period, but we are able to muster our inner strength and rely on those around us to carry us through.[1]

Sometimes stress and depression make us seek outside help; many times, those around us are unaware that we are suffering.

But sometimes things go awry. A state of upheaval occurs: We are literally overloaded. We short-circuit. The stress or depression becomes overwhelming, and we enter what is called a "crisis."[2]

A person who enters a crisis usually does so within about ten days after the stressful event occurs; the crisis may be short-lived, or it may last up to three months or longer. Six weeks seems to be the turning point: You'll be able to tell at that point whether the crisis is going to pass or whether the person will need intensive help in reestablishing equilibrium.[3] Remember: Just as a crisis can bring upheaval, so it can provide an opportunity for growth if handled properly.[4]

> . . . a crisis is a state in which people have failed to resolve a problem, are in disequilibrium, and exhibit the first four out of five characteristics of crisis—symptoms of stress, attitude of panic or defeat, focus upon relief, and decreased efficiency. The fifth characteristic, limited duration, will not be determined for a particular crisis until the crisis is over.[5]
>
> Douglas A. Puryear

A person can grow through a crisis if he has developed inner strength and coping skills. This makes him feel stronger, more perceptive, more competent.[6]

Edgar N. Jackson

Very few people get through life without some personal or family crisis.[7]

Clara Clarkson Park and Leon N. Shapiro

No one is immune from crisis, although some people are more crisis-prone than others. A person who goes through a crisis is *not* mentally ill—crisis is not a disease state.

An individual's ability to cope depends on six major sources of support:[8] intellectual functions, including the ability to solve problems and make decisions; interpersonal assets, including the ability to rely on others for help; emotional resources and an ability to face one's own problems; an attitude of hope, giving the individual a reason for living; a deep motivation to solve one's own problems; and basic personality traits that encourage the individual to cope during difficulty.

The list that follows details some specific personality traits of those who are able to cope effectively as well as the personality traits of those who are crisis-prone.

Good Coping Skills (Able to Withstand Stress)
- Able to orient rapidly to change
- Able to plan and act decisively
- Able to utilize problem-solving mechanisms
- Gets help from external resources, understands increased dependency needs
- Able to deal with emotional aspects of stress while working on the confronting tasks
- Expresses pain and grief freely, saving psychic energy to deal with the environmental challenge
- Can face anticipatory crises and begins to work them out before they happen
- Can tolerate uncertainty
- Appreciates challenges and solves problems, regarding both as a chance to enhance personal growth
- Avoids using self-destructive defenses in dealing with anxieties
- Able to handle loss partly due to the free expression of pain and grief

Poor Coping Skills (Vulnerable to Stress)

- Rapidly disoriented by change
- Suffers from stress—unable to deal with it so it gets the upper hand
- Unable to make decisions
- History of frequent crises ineffectively resolved because of poor coping ability
- Cannot seek help or utilize personal, family, and social supports that might help in coping with stress
- Unable to face reality—denies or avoids reality to an excessive degree by withdrawal or retreating into fantasy
- Acts impulsively when faced with uncertainty (doing without thinking)
- Difficulty in learning from experiences
- Ventilates anger on weaker, vulnerable, or powerless relatives who allow themselves to be used as scapegoats
- Clings desperately, which may annoy and drive away potential support, or avoids others, suggesting to others that the individual doesn't want or need help
- Denies or overcontrols emotions, which leads to eventual eruptions of suppressed feelings
- May develop the "hopelessness–helplessness–giving up" syndrome
- May resort to ritualistic behavior, which serves little or no purpose
- Rest–work cycle disrupted due to inevitable fatigue of crisis state
- May turn to drugs, alcohol, or compulsive food intake to reduce pain
- Cannot ask for help and cannot use it when offered

ELEMENTS OF A CRISIS SITUATION

There are four recognizable stages or elements of a crisis state:[9]

1. *The Hazardous event.*   The occurrence that initiates the chain of reactions leading to a crisis might be one of many normal developmental changes that cause stress, for they require the individual to assume new roles, to learn new tasks, or to adjust to new conditions. The hazardous event might also be a very sudden change, such as sudden loss, a serious illness, accident, or death. While any kind of hazardous event precipitates a crisis, the sudden event causes the most active crisis.[10]

> Something terrible happens, and nobody is to blame.
>
> Robert Frost's definition of tragedy

2. The Vulnerable state.   A person's perceptions and reactions to a hazardous event, the vulnerable state might be one of high anxiety when the hazardous event is perceived as threatening; it might be depression when the event is viewed as a loss; or it might be moderate anxiety and new energy for problem-solving when the hazardous event is perceived as a challenge.

3. Precipitating factor.   The precipitating factor is the final stress-provoking blow that converts a vulnerable state into a state of crisis. The precipitating factor could be as simple as a washing machine breaking down or as complex as the discovery of an unwanted pregnancy.

4. State of active crisis.   A state of active crisis is characterized by an inability to cope with everyday tasks. Although crisis offers a hazard that may lead to a return to a lower level of coping than before the crisis, the process may also be an opportunity to return to a higher level of coping than before. People are most motivated to make life changes when they are in crisis.

COMMON PRECIPITATING EVENTS

Crises are precipitated by physical and psychosocial events that in some way present an overwhelming challenge to a person's coping abilities.[11] Crises may be foreseen or unforeseen; in both instances, the person is overwhelmed by events that are strange, different, or unfamiliar.

Predictable crises.   A crisis is predictable if it is part of the planned, expected, or normal processes of life. Predictable crises range from the normal developmental crises (childhood learning tasks, making the transition from adolescence to young adulthood, retirement, and so on) to such events as a new job, a school examination, or elective surgery. Developmental crises that are particularly stressful include marriage, retirement, and pregnancy. Crises that can be anticipated lend themselves to planning and assurance of intervention.

Unpredictable crises.   Presenting an extraordinary challenge, unpredictable crises fall into various categories of situational stress, such as a natural catastrophe, an unexpected event, or the sudden loss of a bodily function. Major types of unpredictable crises include:[12]

1. Crime victimization
2. Natural disaster (fire, flood, explosion, earthquake, tornado, and so on)
3. Learning of the unexpected death or injury of a family member
4. Accident
5. Psychotic reactions
6. Suicides and attempted suicides
7. Unexpected or tragic family life experience (sudden gain or loss of status or goods, threat of or actual departure of a family member, addition of a member to the family, and demoralization or negative change in the moral position of a family member)

INTERNAL AND EXTERNAL RESOURCES (SUPPORT SYSTEMS)

Coping involves the process of protecting and maintaining emotional stability during stressful situations. To a great extent the success of coping efforts depends upon internal and environmental support systems that have been developed or are available for an individual's use.

The best-known components of a well-developed support system include:

1. Self-esteem: A positive self-image lends the inner sense of competence necessary to deal with the environment.
2. Perception of events: While one person views an event as catastrophic and disastrous, another sees it as an exciting adventure or opportunity for growth.
3. Social network: The greatest support is the family; others the individual may rely on include friends, members of the ethnic group, or, on a larger basis, members of the surrounding larger culture.
4. Coping mechanisms: Constructive mechanisms for coping include the ability to seek accurate information, taking the time to make sound decisions, and maintaining independence.
5. Socioeconomic resources: A buffer against anxiety can be provided by factors such as money, medical attention, education, and economic security.

We all deal with many problems and many threats or potential threats to our security every day. Often we deal with them so easily and quickly that we hardly notice them. To do so we have each developed our particular set of coping mechanisms, those ways in which we typically resolve problems, maintain equilibrium, and thus protect and maintain our security.[13]

Douglas A. Puryear

RECOGNIZING CRISIS REACTIONS

Reactions to emotional crises take many forms. Obvious behavior includes shouting, crying, gesticulating, or otherwise behaving in a highly emotional manner. But some people signal emotional crisis by showing apathetic and depressed behavior that contrasts markedly with a previous pattern of activity and lively interest in family, friends, and work. Sometimes it is even possible to "sense" a person in a vulnerable emotional state because his or her response to interaction is not quite as confident or active as would be expected.

The responses of a person who is experiencing crisis are not the same as those that would occur if he or she were under stress but able to maintain equilibrium. Crisis reactions are often exaggerations of the kinds of responses that normally occur in a noncrisis stress situation.[14]

Depression.   As discussed in Chapter Three, depression is a natural psychological response to loss. Unless depression is recognized and helped early, it may progress to more serious mental and physical problems.[15]

Depressed individuals express feelings of worthlessness and guilt, as well as extreme pessimism. They may want to be left alone, asserting that no one understands or cares about them and that their problems are unsolvable anyway. They usually feel worst in the mornings. When they speak, their conversation may be halting and retarded, as if they hardly had the energy to get the words out.[16]

Anger.   Anger is a natural and expected reaction to crisis. The degree of anger felt and the ways in which it is expressed are related to many things.

Often people respond to discomfort or limitation of function by becoming resentful and suspicious of those around them. They may vent this anger by becoming impatient and irritable or excessively demanding. It is important to realize that their anger stems from fear and discomfort and is not really directed at anyone in particular.

The violently angry person is ready to fight with anyone who approaches and may appear (and may be!) a very formidable adversary. Don't try to force someone in this state to do something against his or her will. Remember that anger and aggressive behavior may simply be the individual's way of dealing with feelings of helplessness.

Guilt.   Guilt is a frequent occurrence both among persons who suffer loss and those who are spared: We all experience to some degree the uneasiness that accompanies sudden and unexplainable good fortune or wonder why we have been spared misfortune when others have suffered.

Some of guilt's many disguises include family quarrels, fear of developing close relationships, and difficulty in expressing emotions.[17]

Grief and mourning.[18]   Grief is an emotional response that follows the recognition of the loss of a valued person or object. It can take the form of feelings of helplessness, hopelessness, loneliness, sadness, guilt, and anger. Mourning is the psychological response that follows the actual loss of a loved one; it includes the processes a person must go through in order to return to a normal emotional state of being.

The normal grief syndrome comprises three stages that occur in the following predictable sequence:[19]

1. *Shock or disbelief.* Lasting from a few minutes to a day or so, a period of shock is characterized by the refusal to believe that the loss has occurred. The person may sit in a daze, motionless, unable to move.

2. *Awareness.* Gradually—usually within hours, minutes, or seconds after the initial shock—the individual realizes what has happened and begins to deal with the reality of the situation. During this period the person experiences anger and denial, lashing out at others he or she perceives as being somehow "responsible" for the loss.

3. *Resolution and reorganization.* Within about one year after the loss occurs, the individual reorders his or her life and begins functioning independently of the lost person or object.

Normal grief that follows this ordered sequence requires no medical treatment; when mourning has served its purpose, it will end spontaneously. People who avoid the necessary process of grief and mourning may, on the other hand, develop psychopathological problems that require treatment.

Confusion, disorganization, and disorientation.   The disorganized person is characterized by uncontrolled and disconnected thought, and usually has incoherent or rambling speech, although he or she may be oriented to person and place. The disoriented person does not know where he or she is or what day it is, and may not even know his or her own name. Often such persons are found wandering aimlessly down the center of a street, dressed peculiarly, and uttering meaningless words and sentences. Confusion can be increased by the presence of unfamiliar people, surroundings, and equipment that may overwhelm the person.

This kind of disturbance is more common among the elderly, who may lapse into memories and behave as if they were still living during an earlier period of their lives. Disorientation may also be a sign of a variety of physical problems, including head injury, reaction to drugs or medication, and metabolic disorders.

> When a person is broken by a crisis, it appears that his inner strength and skills for adjustment are not adequate to meet a new and demanding life experience.[20]
>
> Edgar N. Jackson

Apathy.   Apathy is common among persons who have suffered significant losses of possessions, their homes, friends, or neighbors during a catastrophe. Apathy is also common in the elderly who relocate to new homes or to an institution. There is an all-too-real feeling that they will never be able to recover or replace their losses—there simply does not seem to be enough time, opportunity, or energy to regenerate social and economic resources.

Fear.   During crises many persons suffer realistic fears such as fear of pain, disability, death, or economic hardship. Persistent fears found among young children are often enhanced by vivid imaginations.

Anxiety.[21]   Anxiety often stems from a feeling of helplessness. Nearly all people in crisis feel that they have lost a degree of control over their own existence; furthermore, they must place themselves in the hands of others, often strangers, on whom they must depend completely and whose knowledge and ability they cannot really evaluate. Those individuals whose self-esteem depends on being active, independent, and aggressive are particularly anxious in such a situation.

   Anxiety is increased by unfamiliar people and situations. Often fears can be allayed by support from a familiar person.[22]

Paranoia.   Paranoid people are suspicious, seclusive, and distrustful; they are often hostile and uncooperative and commonly have delusions that others are out to get them. They tend to brood over real or imagined injustices, carry grudges, and recall wrongs experienced years before. Many paranoid persons are easily provoked and unpredictable, and are given to outbursts of bizarre and aggressive behavior. Their personalities are such that they often elicit feelings of dislike or anger in others.

Regression.   Regression involves a return to an earlier or more primitive mode of functioning. A person in crisis must, in certain respects, resume the role of a child, for, like a child, he or she must depend on others for survival.[23]

Denial.   Many persons attempt to ignore their problem, especially in the case of medical illness, because of the anxiety it engenders. Denial is often evident in a tendency to dismiss all symptoms with words such as "only" or "a little."

Self-destructive behavior (suicide).[24]   Suicide is defined as any willful act designed to bring an end to one's own life. The tenth leading cause of death in the United States, it is the third leading cause of death among the fifteen- to twenty-five-year-old group, and the fourth leading cause of death among those between the ages of twenty-five and forty-five. Suicide predominates among men, especially those who are single, widowed, or divorced. The risk of suicide is also higher among depressed persons and alcoholics. Notably, at least 60 percent of all successful suicides have a history of a previous attempt, and three-quarters have given some clear warning of their intentions.

Suicide attempts typically occur when close emotional attachments are endangered or when a significant individual in the person's life has been lost. The suicidal person, in addition, often feels unable to manage his or her own life; a sense of worthlessness and lack of self-esteem are common. Every suicidal act or gesture must be taken seriously.

> . . . not all crises are the same. Some are small and easily managed. Others overwhelm us with the demands they place on our skills to adjust and to adapt to new circumstances.[25]
>
> Edgar N. Jackson

EFFECTING CHANGE IN CRISIS

The primary goal of crisis intervention is to quickly and constructively change the conditions of the persons in crisis.[26]

Ask, "How can we resume function?" Don't ask, "Why did this happen?" Don't try to determine who is right or wrong or attempt to make value judgments; act quickly and assume a nonjudgmental stance or attitude toward the individual in crisis and the circumstances that surround the upset.

Emotional first aid implies urgency. The individual experiencing anxiety, tension, and the out-of-control feelings associated with the crisis state is crying out (directly and indirectly) for immediate attention and relief from distress. If first aid is delayed, the individual may become increasingly upset to the point of disability or self-destruction. As someone helping a person in crisis, your first concerns are to help relieve anxiety and guilt, prevent further disorganization, and protect the person from self-destructive acts or from injuring others. Try the following:

1. Present a calm, reassuring warmth in contrast to the individual's panic. If the emotional feelings are too intense for you to handle, don't abandon the person; get appropriate professional help.
2. Regardless of what the individual may do or say, don't overreact.

3. Reassure the individual that his or her increased dependency needs are legitimate and not shameful.
4. Intervene with action. Do something! Action may involve arranging for immediate physical concerns such as housing, clothing, or simply setting up another counseling appointment. If you are not qualified to handle the problem, refer the person to the proper channel and follow up.
5. Do not make false assurances but communicate hope, concern, and confidence about an eventual successful outcome. The person does not need a promise that things will work out, but rather a sincere offer for help in dealing with reality.

We grow through crises. As we develop skills in making choices and living with them once they are made, we are better able to face the future.[27]

Edgar N. Jackson

Phases of Crisis Intervention

The methods used to accomplish change in crisis will vary depending upon your personal intervention skills and the scene of intervention. It makes a difference in priorities, for example, if intervention takes place at a car accident or in a family crisis at home, if firearms are present, and so on. Crisis intervention involves ten basic phases:[28]

1. *Intervene immediately.* There is a danger that any crisis may result in serious emotional stress, trauma, or other responses such as impaired function, anxiety, diagnosed mental illness, or self-destructive behavior. On the other hand, such a situation is also an opportunity to provide the needed emotional support that can help relieve or resolve the crisis. Immediate intervention is very necessary to prevent disastrous outcomes.

2. *Manipulate the environment.* To the person in crisis, the environment appears overwhelming, confusing, and unmanageable. By controlling environmental factors, you decrease overwhelming, strange, or confusing situations and keep yourself and your actions from adding to the stress and anxiety that might aggravate the crisis. By simply moving the individual to a quiet area, away from all noise, confusion, and disarray, you have decreased the scope of the problem that has to be dealt with.[29]

3. *Assess the individual.* Although the most important role in helping someone in crisis may be to just listen, you also must assess the individual's response and coping capabilities in order to determine how best to help.

As part of this assessment, watch for general appearance (neat and orderly or disheveled?), ability to speak, attention span, ability to communicate with others, memory, mood (fearful? worried?), and thought order—watch out for someone who is having delusions, hallucinations, or serious disturbances in judgment. Evaluate the person's risk of committing suicide or homicide.[30]

4. *Initiate action.* When a crisis arises in someone's life, things need to happen right away toward resolving the crisis. People in a crisis situation tend to be immobilized; help them get moving in a purposeful, coordinated, and goal-directed manner.

5. *Formulate a limited goal.* The goal of crisis intervention is to restore the person experiencing crisis to equilibrium at the same or a higher level of functioning; working through a crisis and reestablishing equilibrium should result in some personal growth.

Formulate long- and short-range goals with the person in mind to reestablish equilibrium. Initially, the short-range goals may be oriented toward averting a catastrophe such as self-destructive behavior, but later goals may focus on less demanding and more growth-promoting aspects of the person's life.

6. *Foster hope and expectations.* People in crisis feel hopeless; foster hope through your attitude toward the person and through the help you render.

7. *Assess the support system.* Assess the coping skills of the individual. What coping mechanisms has he or she used in the past? What personal resources are exhibited? What external resources are available (church, school, friends, family)? How well does the person handle living at present? Determine the degree of disruption, the person's strengths, and other people who may be utilized as supports.

8. *Promote a good self-image.* People in crisis most generally have a low or bad self-image that may stem from feelings of guilt or incapability. This poor self-image can result in the person's feeling angry and belligerent.

To promote a better self-image, treat the person with courtesy and respect, show interest in the nonproblem areas of the person's life, make sure others don't attack or undermine the person's self-esteem, and let the person do as much as possible to relieve the crisis.

9. *Assist in self-reliance.* Persons who experience crisis often manifest regressive tendencies, reverting to an earlier period in life when the situation was more comfortable and less threatening. Urge the person to do as much as he or she can successfully accomplish alone.

10. *Listen.* Listen to the person with three ears—two ears to hear the words spoken, and a third ear to sense the speaker's feelings and meaning.

> Although humans have a drive to grow, any tendency to change is threatening to the security of the system.[31]
>
> Douglas A. Puryear

Notes

[1]John B. Schultz. *Emergency Department Drug Abuse Treatment Technician's Booklet.* Rockville, Md.: National Institute on Drug Abuse, 1978.

[2]*Crisis Intervention.* Distributed by Department of Human Development and Services, UCLA Extension.

[3]Ibid.

[4]Schultz.

[5]Douglas A. Puryear. *Helping People in Crisis.* San Francisco: Jossey-Bass, 1979, p. 11.

[6]Edgar N. Jackson. *Coping with the Crises in Your Life.* New York: Hawthorn, 1974, p. 3.

[7]Clara Claiborn Park and Leon N. Shapiro. *You Are Not Alone.* Boston: Little, Brown, 1976, back cover.

[8]*Comprehensive Emergency Services Training Guide,* 2nd ed. Washington, D.C.: National Center for Comprehensive Emergency Services to Children, U. S. Department of Health, Education and Welfare, DHEW Publication No. (ODHS) 77-30121, 1977.

[9]Ibid.

[10]*Crisis Intervention.*

[11]Gabriel Smilkstein. "The Family in Trouble—How to Tell," *The Journal of Family Practice,* 2, no. 1 (1975), pp. 19–24; Schultz; Morton Bard. *Family Crisis Intervention: From Concept to Implementation.* Washington, D.C.: U. S. Department of Justice, December 1973.

[12]Bard.

[13]Puryear, p. 5.

[14]Schultz.

[15]*Training Manual for Human Service Workers in Major Disasters.* Washington, D.C.: U. S. Department of Health, Education and Welfare; Public Health Service; Alcohol, Drug Abuse, and Mental Health Administration, DHEW Publication No. (ADM) 77-538, 1978.

[16]*EMT—Advanced,* prepublication ed., Washington, D.C.: National Highway Traffic Safety Administration, DOT HS 501207, 1979.

[17]"The Art of Healthy Communication," *Family Health/Today's Health,* July 1977, pp. 25–28.

[18]Hafen, Thygerson, and Rhodes. *Health Perspectives*. Provo, Utah: Brigham Young University Press, 1979, p. 41.

[19]Hafen, Thygerson, and Rhodes; Robert B. White and Leroy T. Gathman. "The Syndrome of Ordinary Grief," *American Family Practitioner*, August 1973, pp. 97–104.

[20]Jackson, p. 3.

[21]*EMT—Advanced*.

[22]National Training Course. *Emergency Medical Technician, Paramedic Instructor's Lesson Plans*, Module XIII, Management of the Emotionally Disturbed. Washington, D.C.: U. S. Department of Transportation, 1977, 0-246-366.

[23]*EMT—Advanced*.

[24]Ibid.

[25]Jackson, p. 3.

[26]*Comprehensive Emergency Services Training Guide*.

[27]Jackson, p. 3.

[28]*Crisis Intervention; EMT—Advanced*; Schultz; *Comprehensive Emergency Services Training Guide*; Brent Hafen and Brenda Peterson. *First Aid for Health Emergencies*. St. Paul: West Publishing Co., 1977; Puryear.

[29]Schultz.

[30]*Crisis Intervention*.

[31]Puryear, p. 30.

chapter five
SEEKING PROFESSIONAL HELP

It's a sad fact of life: It's always easier to recognize other people's problems than it is to face up to our own. You might be expert in recognizing someone else's stress or depression or in deciding when someone else needs help.

Looking inward isn't always such a cinch.

If you noticed yourself shifting uncomfortably as you read the preceding four chapters, it might be time to take on the trying task of assessing whether you need help.

Go through the first four chapters again; if you determine that you are having a real problem consistently coping with the stresses and strains of everyday living, you might consider seeking one of the many avenues of professional help available for emotional support.

KINDS OF PROFESSIONALS
THAT OFFER HELP

A number of different professionals can offer help for emotional problems.[1] The kind of professional you choose should depend on the kind of problem you have and the specific kind of help you need.

Psychiatrist.   A psychiatrist has extensive training: he or she is a medical doctor who has completed a premedical course in an approved university and four years in an accredited medical school, has served one year of hospital internship, and has been a resident for one or more years in some branch of the mental health field. After completing this education and two years of professional experience, he or she must pass an examination given by the American Board of Psychiatry and Neurology before being certified.

A psychiatrist's specialty lies in the diagnosis, treatment, and prevention of emotional and mental disorders. A psychiatrist is needed if there is some kind of physical or medical condition that might accompany the emotional one—a person's emotional problem might result from a brain tumor or from an imbalance in body chemistry, for example. You should also seek out a psychiatrist if you will need therapy that is generally considered to be medical, such as shock therapy or drug therapy. A psychiatrist, because he or she is a medical doctor, is licensed to prescribe medication.

Psychoanalyst.   A psychoanalyst goes through the same gruelling regimen of school and internship/residency as a psychiatrist does—but his or her emphasis is slightly different. While a psychiatrist generally deals in short-term problems and therapies, a psychoanalyst is equipped to handle long-term (sometimes lifelong) problems. The psychoanalyst's brand of therapy is the one most often characterized on steamy television soap operas: He or she delves into the patient's past and tries to uncover old emotional scars that are causing current problems. The course of treatment is usually long and expensive, and can be difficult and painful for the patient; however, it may be recommended for certain kinds of serious conditions that won't respond to other efforts.

Psychologist.   Anyone who has accredited training in psychology—the scientific study of the behavior of man and other animals—comes under the catchall title of *psychologist*. Generally, a clinical psychologist who takes on individual patients must have a doctoral degree in psychology from a recognized school, two years of experience under supervision in a mental health facility, and the successful completion of a national examination of the American Association of State Psychological Boards. It takes almost as long—eight to ten years—to become a psychologist as it does to become a psychiatrist.

The largest area of specialization in psychology is clinical psychology; others include experimental, physiological, comparative, social, industrial, abnormal, developmental, and child psychology.

A psychologist doesn't try to analyze behavior: he or she is more interested in the problem than in its deep-seated causes. A psychologist is trained to give tests that can uncover neurological difficulties that may be related to the emotional problem but cannot prescribe drugs to treat a neurological disorder or any other physical problem. (The psychologist must refer the patient to a psychiatrist or a medical doctor if drugs are needed.)

Psychiatric social workers. A psychiatric social worker doesn't complete the specialized schooling required of psychiatrists and psychologists; instead, he or she receives specialized training in counseling. Most often, a master's degree in social work is completed at an accredited college or university.

A psychiatric social worker can't help you if there are underlying medical problems causing your emotional difficulty or if you need medication as a part of your therapy. If you have no medical problem that might reflect on your emotional problem, a psychiatric social worker can be a good source of emotional counseling.

Psychiatric nurses. A psychiatric nurse receives no advanced degree and is required to pass no certification examination. Most of the time, he or she is a registered nurse who has received a limited amount of training in psychotherapy. Often, a psychiatric nurse is an employee of a hospital who has been assigned to the psychiatric ward and who has to have some understanding of the emotional difficulties of the patients.

Counselor. A counselor is the least trained of all; counselors need no advanced degree and do not need to pass an examination. A counselor may feel qualified to help others because of an inborn talent or because he or she has experienced things that have provided an increased understanding and ability to help. A counselor is usually less expensive than other therapists. While his or her education may be limited, a counselor can often give help when the greatest need is for a listening ear and some sound advice. Of course, a counselor cannot prescribe medication or diagnose or treat medical problems.

A counselor is allowed by law to practice by counseling people just as a psychiatrist or psychologist might, as long as he or she doesn't pretend to have that education or certification.

If you have questions about a certain therapist in your community or if you wonder whether someone can provide the kind of treatment you might require, you can obtain information by writing to one of the following:

American Psychological Association
Office of Professional Affairs
1200 Seventeenth Street, NW
Washington, DC 20036

American Psychiatric Association
1700 Eighteenth Street, NW
Washington, DC 20009

Family Service Association of America
44 East Twenty-third Street
New York, NY 10010

You can also check the *Mental Health Directory*, which lists professionals and their credentials by state. You can get a copy of the directory free of charge from

National Institute of Mental Health
Public Inquiries Office, Room 11-A-33
5600 Fishers Lane
Rockville, MD 20852

ALTERNATIVES
TO A PROFESSIONAL THERAPIST

"Seeking help" doesn't always imply seeking out a professional therapist or counselor—it simply means turning to someone else for help and strength you can't produce on your own. You might consider one of these alternatives to a professional counselor, depending on the nature of your problem:

Clergy. If you belong to a church, you might be aware of counseling services that are offered by your priest, rabbi, or bishop. In some churches, members of the clergy receive some basic training in psychology for this exact reason. They can help if your problem is one that would be solved by an objective observer who could offer some good advice. You don't need to belong to the church in many cases; most members of the clergy are willing to talk to anyone who needs the help. They could be of specific help for problems that have religious or philosophical overtones.

Friends.   A person who knows you, cares about you, and wants the best for you might be the best therapist of all—and a friend or acquaintance might be able to give you the help you need if the problem is not serious and if the friend is not a part of or involved in the problem. If the problem is one that involves the friend, steer clear: You will not receive unbiased advice. You might also discover that the friend is too close to offer objective counsel.

Organized groups.   Group therapy has always been popular because it helps to know you're not alone. Many groups have become skilled at offering help to people with specific problems. Alcoholics Anonymous and Weight Watchers are two examples; this type of group deals with specific problems, of course, so you wouldn't go to Weight Watchers to battle a problem with shyness or fear of heights. The group approach is generally much less expensive (free in some cases), but you won't be able to receive the kind of specialized help that is available from a professional. Again, the nature of your problem can dictate which avenue is best for you.

> A good psychiatrist should be like a good parent; that is, he should eventually become dispensable.
>
> Bennett Olshaker

LICENSING OF PROFESSIONALS

In most states there are government boards and agencies that license professionals to practice in their respective areas. But in some states the push is on to abolish government boards and agencies that apparently serve no useful function—and among the list of agencies on the chopping block are the psychology examining and regulating boards.

Deregulation brings with it certain hazards that you should watch out for if you live in a state that has abolished regulatory agencies. The field can become overrun with unqualified or incompetent practitioners. At best, they may simply be unable to offer you the kind of care you need. At worst, there are more serious problems: They may not follow rules of confidentiality, and medical insurance companies usually don't recognize them, so you'll have to foot the entire bill yourself. (Medicare will not reimburse you if you get help from someone who has not been licensed.)

> Deregulation takes away all protection for the consumer. Once the law goes, the enforcement goes also.
>
> William Barnhill

KINDS OF TREATMENT AVAILABLE

Many different techniques are available to therapists for handling mental and emotional situations. You should remember two important things about treatment: You should receive a treatment that is appropriate for your specific problem, and you should never feel forced or obligated to continue with a treatment you feel uncomfortable about.

When choosing a professional, you should choose one who is licensed to perform the specific kind of treatment you may need. If you need treatment that your professional can't provide, he or she should be willing to refer you to another professional who can be of help.

Psychoanalysis. Originated by Sigmund Freud, psychoanalysis is a long-term process that seeks to interpret what's going on in your unconscious mind. The intense probing common to psychoanalysis seeks to determine the factors that have combined throughout your life to produce the set of problems you now have. The philosophy of psychoanalysis says that by uncovering old emotional scars and helping them heal, new problems and future problems can be eliminated and prevented.

To be legitimate, psychoanalysis must be provided by a psychoanalyst who has been certified by the American Psychoanalytic Association, who is a medical doctor, and who has received specific training.

You need to be especially careful about a person who claims to be a psychoanalyst: For some reason, this title attracts more quacks than any of the other fields in emotional health. Especially common are people who have been psychoanalyzed themselves and who, as a result, feel "qualified" to help others. Insist on seeing certification and proof of required educational training.

Be careful, too, that the psychoanalyst you choose has sound ideas about practice. As with any other profession, there are unethical or disturbed people in psychoanalysis. You should generally steer clear of someone who seems too troubled or disturbed to be of much help or who tries to force you to participate in unconventional, questionable therapy, such as extramarital sex or astrology.

Hypnosis. Hypnosis as a therapy carries with it a great deal of controversy. It relies on achieving a state of increased suggestibility, induced by suggestion, to produce a condition of intense concentration. People who have been hypnotized look like they are asleep, but nothing could be farther from the truth.

Hypnosis can often be used in combination with other kinds of therapy, but it is rarely used alone in treatment. While about 15 percent of the population can put themselves in hypnotic trances, many people can't be hypnotized at all. Why? The ability to be hypnotized doesn't depend on your doctor's skill—it depends on you. A patient who isn't suggestible enough can't be hypnotized, and many factors, such as illness, fear, anger, or preoccupation with other thoughts and emotions can prevent you from achieving the mental condition necessary for hypnosis.

Human sexuality counseling. Masters and Johnson, the pioneering husband/wife team who authored *Human Sexual Inadequacy*, were the professionals who sparked interest in the field that eventually evolved into human sexuality counseling. Sex therapists often work as husband/wife teams and offer help for sexual problems such as difficulty in achieving orgasm, premature ejaculation, impotence, sexual incompetency, and sexual dysfunction.

While human sexuality counseling can be of tremendous help when it is carried out by competent professionals, it carries the hazard of attracting quacks—people who think it sounds like an enticing way of making a living, but who are not trained or licensed to practice. Masters estimates that only 0.1 percent of those practicing have been adequately trained, and suggests that there are approximately 3,500 quack sex therapists practicing in the United States today.[2]

If your problem is a sexual one and you decide to seek help through human sexuality counseling, ask for credentials! A sex therapist must be a psychotherapist (medical doctor with additional training and certification) with at least two years of additional supervised study in human sexuality and the treatment of sexual problems. Because so many sexual problems have medical underpinnings, it is essential that you choose a professional who has the essential medical training. The Reproductive Biology Research Foundation in St. Louis, Missouri, is one of the few sexual research institutes in the United States where sexual therapists are trained.

Because of the intensely personal nature of sex therapy, it takes courage to go through it. Make sure of your doctor's credentials before you undergo any kind of treatment—a first experience that is bizarre or frightening may render you incapable of seeking other, professional help. If you need to find a competent, professional sex therapist, ask your doctor; other sources might include your city or county medical society, your local family or children's services, or your minister, priest, or rabbi.[3]

Marriage counseling.   More than six million Americans are separated or divorced, and the divorce rate has recently risen to one divorce in every 3.5 marriages.[4] There's an obvious need, then, for professional counseling, but, unfortunately, authorities estimate that about half of all those practicing in this country are either incompetent or untrained. The American Association of Marriage Counselors and the Family Service Association estimate that quack counselors bilk gullible couples out of approximately $700 million each year.[5] More devastating than the financial loss, however, is the fact that untrained counselors tend to destroy existing marital relationships rather than to stabilize them.

> Increasingly, married couples are realizing they need help and are going to marriage counselors. What they are often getting are "counselors" who are not trained or qualified to handle their problems. Some are getting advice from the intentionally fraudulent.
>
> Ray Fowler

The goal of marriage counseling is to save and improve the marriage relationship, but successful counseling may still result in a couple who divorces. Generally, marriage counseling is considered successful if the counselor can help the husband and wife resolve personal problems and lead normal, happy lives—even if the marriage itself ends. Personal growth of each of the partners is of importance in counseling.

Marriage counseling, like sexual counseling, attracts plenty of quacks. Currently only three states—California, Michigan, and New Jersey—require counselors to be licensed. There is only one reliable source where you can obtain information about a counselor. Write

> The American Association of Marriage and
>   Family Counselors
> 225 Yale Avenue
> Claremont, CA 91711

You may use a member of the clergy or a social services counselor for marriage counseling as long as you realize that he or she is not trained and may not offer you the kind of help you can get from a professional.

> Choose a counselor as you would a doctor or lawyer. Ask about credentials, training, and years in practice. Check with friends who have been in a similar situation for tips in finding the kind of help you want.
>
> *U.S. News and World Report*

Family counseling.   In family counseling, the entire family is interviewed by the counselor to determine the root of the problem. Sometimes an entire family seeks help to begin with, but most often it is one individual family member. After working with that single family member for a few sessions, the therapist may determine that other members of the family may be contributing to the problem and may also need help.

A son may need to be with his father, who is unavailable in the evenings when the son is home from school. A mother may be spending too much time worrying about things that would be less of a problem if she could see them in perspective. Family therapists try to help family members see each other in a new light. The common result of this is improved behavior on the part of all family members and resolution of the problem that prompted counseling initially.

Group therapy.   Based on many of the same philosophies that have fostered groups like Weight Watchers and Alcoholics Anonymous, group therapy takes place when a small group of people gather to discuss their problems with each other under the guidance of a licensed therapist. The therapist guides the conversation into useful directions while the group members help each other with their individual problems.

The therapist is an essential ingredient in the group therapy situation, not only by guiding the conversation and preventing side-tracking and hostility, but by offering advice and pointing out possibilities that group members might have missed on their own.

One form of group therapy is called *psychodrama*. By playing a role—such as father, mother, sister, or brother—and by creating a scene, the patient can discover personal feelings and reactions to others that were hidden before treatment.

Sometimes groups are composed of people who have the same kind of problem; other therapists choose to mix people with different kinds of problems into one group. There are advantages to each method. People who all have the same kind of problem can share experiences that will be meaningful and can develop genuine empathy. On the other hand, people with different kinds of problems can remain objective enough to offer real help.

Play therapy.   A method used for children, play therapy can help a child who has deep-seated fears, behavior problems, or learning problems. Young children respond best; older children find it more difficult to change behavior through play therapy. A licensed therapist guides a child in various techniques, such as role-playing, to help the child modify his or her feelings and change behavior patterns.

WHERE PATIENTS GO

A great deal of professional help is offered in the counselor's or doctor's office. The patient arrives at the scheduled time of the appointment, meets with the therapist, and returns home after the appointment.

There are a few variations on this theme, and your therapist will decide which will be best for you. The most common include:

Partial hospitalization. If medication or drug therapy is required, you might need to spend part of your time in the hospital. Usually your treatment can be worked out so that you can go to work and live at home while spending either days, nights, or weekends at the hospital.

Outpatient clinic care. While you continue to live at home and to go to work, you are treated at a hospital clinic on a regular basis. For example, you may come to the clinic every day at noon or may come each Monday, Wednesday, and Friday at 3 P.M. for treatment.

Inpatient care. If your problem requires extensive and immediate treatment, you may be hospitalized for a short time so that the therapy can continue around the clock. You may also be hospitalized if your problem requires hospital testing (such as tests conducted to detect a brain tumor) or hospital treatments (usually medical in nature). You may be referred to the hospital emergency room if you become violent or self-destructive; you are then hospitalized to protect yourself and others until you can regain control and function normally with others. While some inpatient care is long and drawn-out, much of it is short-term, sometimes lasting no longer than a week or two.

CHOOSING A PROFESSIONAL

It's critical that you choose the right person. Your ability to be helped depends on the amount of confidence and trust you place in your professional therapist. A therapist who isn't qualified or who is simply not right for you can cause you to leave with more problems than you came in with!

The first step to take is to consider the nature of your problem. A person who needs to overcome the anxiety of taking math examinations might be able to receive excellent help from a counselor; seeking out a psychoanalyst would be foolish, because such extensive treatment is unnecessary and expensive. Someone whose faulty metabolism is causing a wide range of mental and emotional problems, on the other hand, must seek out a professional who can diagnose and treat medical as well as emotional problems, such as a psychoanalyst or psychiatrist.

Once you decide what *kind* of therapist you need, ask around—

even Ann Landers advised her readers in her October 13, 1980, column that the best referral for a mental health professional is a personal recommendation from a satisfied patient. If you have friends or family members who have sought the same kind of help, ask who the therapist was and what kind of treatment was given. If your friend was highly satisfied, ask why; if he or she was unsatisfied, try to find out if it was the therapist's fault.

Regardless of how much someone else liked a therapist, *you* must have confidence if your treatment is to be successful. You should be right for the therapist, and the therapist should be right for you. To find out how you might interact before actually going in for treatment, make an appointment—and *you* do the interviewing. Ask the therapist any question that occurs to you: how the therapist thinks you will be helped, whether he or she has seen others who have similar problems, and how involved the treatment will need to be. (Don't be afraid to talk to two or three therapists. You might be comfortable with one but think that the price is unreasonable; after talking to a few more, you might find out that the price is a standard one.) You might want to ask the therapist about his or her general philosophies.

More important than what the therapist says is how he or she makes you feel—what are your gut instincts? Do you think you could work well with this therapist, or do you feel uncomfortable and strained? Does the therapist mention using therapies that you find unacceptable? If so, keep looking.

You also need to consider the mechanics of the therapy. Is the office or clinic near enough so that you can get to your treatment sessions without undue difficulty? You should look for a therapist who is close to your home, or one that is near your office if you plan to go on your lunch breaks. Choosing a therapist whose office is clear across town can result in a financial burden and a time commitment that is too excessive.

Find out when the therapist sees patients—that can be a determining factor, too. You may need to visit the therapist during certain hours of the day or on certain days of the week so that your therapy won't interfere with your job; you have to find out whether this is possible. Find out also if the therapist will be available on short notice in case of an emergency. Even an excellent therapist who is unavailable during a crisis isn't the best one for you.

Ask about the therapist's credentials. Don't be afraid to ask to see evidence: a license, a diploma, certificates. A professional who is well qualified and who is not making any false claims will be happy to provide you with any background information you want; a quack will probably become agitated and abusive.

A big consideration is the financial one: What does the therapist charge? Can you pay that amount? Therapy usually costs between $15 and $100 an hour, depending on the city you are in and the kind of help you need. You might be able to bargain—some therapists will lower the fee, but only if *you* are the one who suggests it. Find out what the payment arrangements are: Will the office bill you or your insurance company, or must you pay at the completion of each visit? Most therapists require a patient to pay for a missed visit if it was not canceled within a certain time prior to the appointment; find out what that time is. (Some therapists will allow you to call the day before; others require more notification.) If money is a consideration for you, don't be afraid to shop around—compare the prices charged and the terms offered. The financial burden of psychotherapy can become so great that it can result in further emotional problems for you if you agree to a therapist who charges too much. Settle for someone who is willing to work with you and your limited resources—many are genuinely committed to helping people and will adjust their fees if they determine you really need help and can afford only a lesser fee.

PSYCHOQUACKERY

It's a fact of life: Many people who are untrained, unskilled, and unlicensed are out there, waiting to victimize and take advantage of you. They prey on people who have emotional problems, because those people are more vulnerable than they normally would be.

There are plenty of problems that follow the mental health quack. One is financial—it's impossible to estimate how much money is spent (and lost) each year by patients who pay unscrupulous therapists and buy worthless mental health treatments, gadgets, and literature. Even more devastating is the time wasted by these people. Perhaps worst of all is the fact that an unqualified therapist can actually make a situation worse instead of solving the patient's problems.

A 29-year-old woman who tried group therapy with an unlicensed therapist told how, in addition to normal fees, clients had to pay monetary "penance" into a group "kitty" for such infractions as using the bathroom during a session or failing to address oneself to another client's problems.

"The therapist also believed in acting out your anger," she explained. "It was a painful kind of thing, bending people's arms, socking women in the breasts. He did things like that in private sessions, too. He punched me in the breasts, banged my head on the floor, and pulled out my pubic hairs. When I told him I didn't like it, he said I really had a problem with healthy play."

One man learned that his wife was having sex with her therapist— while he sat outside the treatment room waiting for her. "She said that he made her do it and that she was sorry, guilty, and sick," explained the husband. Later, the woman was hospitalized in a mental institution, partly as a result of the sex therapy.

Today's Health

Counseling by unqualified persons often is based on too-simplistic solutions to complex problems. Such counseling is obviously unhelpful and can be harmful to people with marital problems.

Irene Blickstein

Earmarks of a Quack Counselor

To avoid getting caught in the trap of quackery, keep your eye out for the following signs.[6] An unqualified counselor

1. Advertises his or her services flamboyantly, especially in the Yellow Pages of the telephone directory. (Ads often make excessive claims without presenting good evidence and rely on testimonies of former patients.)
2. Offers quick or guaranteed solutions to your problems. (No qualified professional will guarantee you a complete cure, regardless of how simple your problem might be—one may offer a hopeful prognosis, but no guarantees.)
3. Charges excessive fees.
4. Makes hasty diagnoses—sometimes over the telephone—without first sifting out the essential facts.
5. Resents any request for credentials or inquiries into his or her training and experience.

6. Has an intimate or obscene approach.
7. Is unwilling to refer you to someone else, claiming to be all things to all people.
8. Professes to use only one therapeutic approach for all problems.
9. Harps on sex as the underlying reason for all problems.
10. Claims to provide services for which his or her training and experience are clearly inadequate.
11. Makes excessive claims about the results of his or her treatment.
12. Is unwilling to consider that the claimed results might be due to factors he or she has not taken into account.
13. Claims, without evidence, that his or her treatment is more "natural" than others and is not merely "treating symptoms," but is treating the basic cause.
14. Depends on articles in the popular press (by the counselor or others) rather than upon carefully prepared scientific publications.
15. Fails to write letters to the editor requesting clarification and toning-down of claims made in lay articles written by others about his or her treatment.
16. Resorts to threats of litigation when criticized rather than to professional debate.

More important than whether a person is a psychiatrist or a psychologist is whether he can identify with the healthy side of the patient and make that side more and more important. A good therapist is tolerant and understanding and open. And these qualities don't come from a medical school any more than they come from a Ph.D. program. They come from life.

David S. Viscott

There is no quick solution for many emotional problems. Often you will need to search and work to find the solutions—but it is time and effort well spent. With the right kind of therapist to help you, your chances for recovery are good.

The first step—that of seeking help—takes courage, but it leads to opportunities beyond your imagination. So go ahead—take the first step. With each step that you take, the next will become a little easier, until you are clear and free and fully healthy.

The personal qualities of the individual therapist are much more important than the letters after his name. Having a diploma isn't enough. What really matters is the ability of the therapist and the patient to get along. The relationship is the basic tool of psychotherapy.

                                                          Melvin A. Gravitz

Notes

[1]"How to Pick the Right Therapist," *Consumer's Digest*, May/June 1981, pp. 38–39; "Psychological Mayhem," *Today's Health*, February 1974.

[2]William H. Masters. "Phony Sex Clinics—Medicine's Newest Nightmares," *Today's Health*, November 1974.

[3]Ibid.

[4]David Shaw. "What Happens When You Open Up to a Marriage Counselor," *Today's Health*, November 1973.

[5]Jack Kaplan. "Frauds Who Prey on Shaky Marriages," *Today's Health*, June 1969.

[6]Jack Kaplan and Barbara J. Katz. "Finding Psychiatric Help Can Be Traumatic Itself," *The National Observer*, December 16, 1972.

INDEX